D1150042

HAMLYN POCKET GUIDES

FRENCH

PHRASE BOOK
AND DICTIONARY

HAMLYN POCKET GUIDES

FRENCH

PHRASE BOOK
AND DICTIONARY

compiled by

LEXUS

with Sophie Marin

HAMLYN

First published 1989 by
The Hamlyn Publishing Group Limited
Michelin House, 81 Fulham Road
LONDON SW3 6RB

Second impression 1989

ISBN 0 600 56430 4

Printed in Great Britain

INTRODUCTION

This new phrase book and dictionary has been designed to combine a large number of features in a single integrated package.

A total of 101 concise sections, arranged in alphabetical order, give you information on how to deal with a variety of situations in French. Flicking through the book and looking at the headings at the tops of the pages will give you an instant guide to the contents list.

There are sections for activities such as shopping, driving, changing money, buying a ticket, ordering a meal etc.

There are sections which enable you to express reactions, to express your feelings, likes, dislikes, emotions etc. Sections for making requests, for talking about yourself and for understanding people.

And the nuts and bolts of the language are clearly presented in straightforward grammar sections so that you can go further with your French and develop some skill in the language.

And for deciphering French signs a comprehensive list of things you're likely to see when travelling abroad has been included — in addition to a menu reader and drinks list. And as well as this a number of typical responses that you might get from French people if you say something or ask a question in French have been included.

All the phrases are provided with an easy-to-use pronunciation guide (see below) and there are also guidelines on the pronunciation of French.

And so that you can build up your French vocabulary and make modifications to the phrases given in the various sections, this book also includes a 3,000 word dictionary of English into French.

Some notes on the pronunciation system used

The pronunciation guide in this book is based on
writing out French words as though they were English
words. So if you read out the pronunciation line as
English you will communicate with a French person.
(For more information on French pronunciation, see
PRONUNCIATION). Some special conventions
have been used.

añ	a French nasal sound – the n is not actually pronounced; for example, say the word 'sang' leaving off the ng and speaking nasally and you are near
ew	the French u sound described under *PRONUNCIATION*
ī	like the i sound in 'tie' or 'cry'
j	like the s sound in 'measure' or the z sound in 'seizure'
oñ, om̃	nasal sounds – the n/m are not actually pronounced; say 'on' leaving off the n and speaking nasally and you are near

Notes on translations

In most cases 'you' has been translated by the polite
form **vous**. In some cases, however, two translations
have been given. The first is the familiar **tu** form and
the second the polite **vous** form. For more on this see
PRONOUNS.

An **e** in brackets indicates the feminine form of a word
(see *ADJECTIVES*).

ACCEPTING, SAYING YES

Yes please.
Oui, s'il vous plaît.
wee seel voo play

Thank you.
Merci.
mairsee

Yes, I'd like to.
Oui, je veux bien.
wee juh vuh b-yān

Yes, that would be very nice.
Oui, ça serait formidable.
wee sa suhray formeedahbl

Ok, fine.
Oui, d'accord.
wee dakor

I'd love one, I'd love to.
Je veux bien.
juh vuh b-yān

I'll take two.
J'en prends deux.
jōn prōn duh

That's just right thanks.
C'est parfait, merci.
say parfay mairsee

Great!, good idea!
Très bien, quelle bonne idée !
tray b-yān kel bon eeday

ADJECTIVES

In French, adjectives have to 'agree' with the noun they are used with. This means that, if a noun is feminine, then an adjective used with it must be in the feminine form too. If a noun is plural then an adjective used with it must be in the plural form too, masculine or feminine. In the dictionary section of this book all adjectives are translated by the masculine form, the form used with nouns preceded by **un** or **le**.

For most adjectives, the feminine form is made by adding **-e**. And the plural is formed in two ways: for those with masculine nouns — by adding **-s**; and for those with feminine nouns by adding **-es**.

Plurals for adjectives ending in **-au** are usually formed by adding **-x** (although the **-s/-x** are not pronounced).

The feminine of adjectives ending in **-eux** is formed by changing **-eux** to **-euse**.

Important exceptions are shown in the dictionary section.

Here are some examples of adjective endings:

Je suis heureux.
juh swee ur-ruh
I am happy. (said by man)

Je suis heureuse.
juh swee ur-rurz
I am happy. (said by woman)

Un ordinateur français.
an ordeenatur frõnsay
A French computer.

Une voiture française.
ewn vwatewr frõnsez
A French car.

Deux ordinateurs américains.
duh zordeenatur amayreekãn
Two American computers.

Deux voitures américaines.
duh vwatewr amayreeken
Two American cars.

Note that most adjectives in French, as in these examples, are placed after the noun, not in front of it as in English.

But some common adjectives are put in front of nouns:

beau	*bo*	beautiful
bon	*bõn*	good
joli	*jolee*	pretty
mauvais	*movay*	bad
gentil	*jõntee*	nice
nouveau	*noovo*	new
grand	*grõn*	big
petit	*puhtee*	little
jeune	*jurn*	young
vieux	*v-yuh*	old

AGREEING WITH PEOPLE

That's right.
Oui, c'est ça.
wee say sa

No no, you're quite right.
Non non, vous avez raison.
noñ noñ voo zavay rezzoñ

Oh yes.
Oh oui.
o wee

That's just what I think.
C'est bien ce que je pense.
say b-yañ suh kuh juh poñss

Absolutely.
Tout à fait.
toota fay

You were right.
Vous aviez raison.
voo zavee-ay rezzoñ

He agrees with me.
Il est d'accord avec moi.
eel ay dakor avek mwah

So do /am I.
Moi aussi.
mwa o-see

Nor do /am I.
Moi non plus.
mwa noñ plew

ALPHABET

The alphabet in French is pronounced as follows:

a *ah*
b *bay*
c *say*
d *day*
e *uh*
f *ef*
g *jay*
h *ash*
i *ee*
j *jee*
k *ka*
l *el*
m *em*
n *en*
o *o*
p *pay*
q *kew*
r *air*
s *ess*
t *tay*
u *ew*
v *vay*
w *doobl-vay*
x *eex*
y *ee-grek*
z *zed*

To spell your name, Harris, in French you would say:
ash-ah-air-air-ee-ess

When writing French, accents are normally omitted on capital letters.

See also the section on *PRONUNCIATION*.

ANNOYANCE

Bother! Damn!
Mince alors ! Zut !
mānss alor zewt

It's very annoying.
C'est très embêtant.
say tray zōmbetōn

That's totally impossible.
C'est totalement impossible.
say totahl-mōn ōmposseebl

Don't be silly.
Ne soyez pas ridicule.
nuh swī-yay pa reedeekewl

Rubbish!
N'importe quoi !
nōmport kwa

Of course not!
Bien sûr que non !
b-yōn sewr kuh nōn

What do you expect!
Qu'est-ce que vous croyez ?
keskuh voo krwī-ay

Oh come on now!
Allons !
alōn

You idiot!
Quel idiot !
kel eed-yo

APOLOGIES

Sorry.
Pardon.
pardon

I'm very sorry.
Je suis vraiment désolé.
juh swee vraymon dayzolay

RESPONSES

Je vous en prie.
juh voo zon pree
That's ok.

Cela n'a pas d'importance.
suhla na pa damportonss
It doesn't matter.

He says he's very sorry.
Il vous demande de l'excuser.
eel voo duhmonde duh lex-kewzay

Please accept my apologies.
Je vous prie de bien vouloir m'excuser.
juh voo pree duh b-yan voolwahr mex-kewzay

I feel awful.
Je suis vraiment très ennuyé.
juh swee vraymon tray zonwee-ay

I'll buy you another one.
Je vous le/la remplacerai.
juh voo luh/la romplasseray

ARTICLES

French has three words for 'the':

le	*luh*	— for masculine singular nouns
la	*la*	— for feminine singular nouns
les	*lay*	— for all plural nouns

In front of a noun beginning with a vowel (or an 'h' that is not pronounced) **le** and **la** change to **l'**.

Le bus.	**La chambre.**
luh bewss	*la shōmbr*
The bus.	The room.

Les Français.	**L'hôtel.**
lay frōnsay	*lohtel*
The French.	The hotel.

The equivalents for saying 'a' are:

un	*ān*	— for masculine nouns
une	*ewn*	— for feminine nouns

Un bus.	**Une chambre.**
ān bewss	*ewn shōmbr*
A bus.	A room.

If you are using **le/les** with **de** (of; from) make the following changes:

de + le = du *dew*
de + les = des *day*

With **à** (to; at) make these changes:

à + le = au *o*
à + les = aux *o*

ASKING QUESTIONS

There are three main ways of forming questions in French.

1   You can simply give your voice a questioning tone and leave the sequence of words just as they would be in a statement:

   Il est là.
   eel ay la
   He's there.

   Il est là?
   eel ay la
   Is he there?

2   You can use the words **est-ce que** in front of the subject leaving the rest of the sentence in the normal word order for a statement:

   David est sorti.
   daveed ay sortee
   David has gone out.

   Est-ce que David est sorti?
   eskuh daveed ay sortee
   Has David gone out?

3   You can invert the order of subject and verb:

   Elle est partie.
   el ay partee
   She has left.

   Est-elle partie?
   ay-tel partee
   Has she left?

ATTENTION: GETTING PEOPLE'S ATTENTION

Excuse me!
Excusez-moi, s'il vous plaît !
ex-kewzay-mwa seel voo play

Hello!
S'il vous plaît !
seel voo play

Waiter!
Garçon, s'il vous plaît !
garsoñ seel voo play

Waitress!
Mademoiselle, s'il vous plaît !
mad-mwazel seel voo play

Miss!
Mademoiselle, s'il vous plaît !
mad-mwazel seel voo play

Is there anyone there?
Est-ce qu'il y a quelqu'un ?
eskeel ya kelkañ

Hoy you!
Hé, vous !
ay voo

> **Monsieur, s'il vous plaît !**
> *muh-sewr seel voo play*
> Excuse me!

> **Madame, s'il vous plaît !**
> *ma-dam seel voo play*
> Excuse me!

BANKS

Can I change this into francs?
Puis-je changer cet argent en francs ?
pwee-juh shōnjay set arjōn ōn frōn

I want to draw cash on this credit card.
Je voudrais retirer de l'argent avec ma carte de crédit.
juh voodray ruhteeray duh larjōn avek ma kart duh kraydee

I'd like to cash these traveller's cheques.
Est-ce que je peux changer ces traveller's chèques ?
eskuh juh puh shōnjay say traveler shek

Can I cash this cheque here?
Puis-je toucher ce chèque ici ?
pwee-juh tooshay suh shek ee-see

This is the phone number of my bank at home.
Voilà le numéro de téléphone de ma banque.
vwala luh newmayro duh taylayfon duh ma bōnk

> **Combien voulez-vous changer ?**
> *kōmb-yān voolay-voo shōnjay*
> How much do you want to change?

> **Puis-je voir votre passeport ?**
> *pwee-juh vwahr votr pass-por*
> Can I have your passport?

> **Passez à la caisse prendre votre argent.**
> *passay a la kess prōndr votr arjōn*
> You get your money at the cash desk.

Can you give me some small change as well?
Pouvez-vous aussi me donner de la monnaie ?
poovay-voo o-see muh donnay duh la monnay

Can you change this into smaller notes?
Pouvez-vous me faire la monnaie ?
poovay-voo muh fair la monnay

BEACH, THE POOL

Let's go down to the beach.
Allons à la plage.
alon za la plahj

I'm going to the pool.
Je vais à la piscine.
juh vay ala pee-seen

They're on the beach.
Ils sont sur la plage.
eel son sewr la plahj

Can we have a beach umbrella?
Pouvons-nous avoir un parasol ?
poovon-noo zavvwahr an parasol

Where do you get the towels from?
Où est-ce qu'on trouve ces serviettes ?
oo eskuh on troov say sairvee-et

Can I have a recliner?
Puis-je avoir une chaise longue ?
pwee-juh avvwahr ewn shez lon-g

Are you coming in?
Vous venez vous baigner ?
voo vuhnay voo ben-yay

I can't swim.
Je ne sais pas nager.
juh nuh say pa na-jay

> **Baignade interdite**
> No bathing

> **Baignade surveillée**
> Lifeguards on beach

BUSES

Which bus goes to ...?
Quel bus va à ... ?
kel bewss va a

Does this bus go to ...?
Est-ce que ce bus va à ...?
eskuh suh bewss va a

When's the next bus to ...?
Quand part le prochain bus pour ...?
koñ par luh proshen bewss poor

Is there a bus that goes there?
Est-ce qu'il y a un bus qui va là ?
eskeel ya añ bewss kee va la

What time does the bus go back?
A quelle heure le bus revient ?
a kel urr luh bewss ruhv-yañ

When does the last bus leave?
A quelle heure part le dernier bus ?
a kel urr par luh dairn-yay bewss

A single to ...
Un aller pour ...
añ alay poor

Two returns to ...
Deux aller-retours pour ...
duh zalay-ruhtoor poor

Could you tell me when to get off?
Pouvez-vous me dire où je dois descendre ?
poovay-voo muh deer oo juh dwa duh-soñdr

> **Arrêt de bus**
> Bus stop

BUSINESS TRAVEL

I'm here on business.
Je suis ici pour affaires.
juh swee ee-see poor afair

James O'Connor to see Mr/Mrs/Miss ...
James O'Connor, je suis venu voir
Monsieur/Madame/Mademoiselle ...
James O'Connor juh swee vuhnew vwahr muh-sewr/madam/mad-mwazel

My company is ...
Ma société s'appelle ...
ma sosee-aytay sapel

I'll wait.
Je vais attendre.
juh vay atōndr

Do you have a card?
Avez-vous une carte ?
avay-voo ewn kart

We'd like to get this firmed up.
Nous voudrions conclure cette affaire.
noo voodree-ōn kōnklewr set affair

Can you give us more time?
Nous avons besoin de plus de temps.
noo zavōn buhzwān duh plewss duh tōm

I'll get them faxed over.
Je vais les envoyer par fax.
juh vay lay zōnvwi-yay par fax

It's a pleasure doing business with you.
C'est un plaisir de travailler avec vous.
say tān plezzeer duh travi-yay avek voo

CAMPING

Excuse me, do you know where the nearest campsite is?
Excusez-moi, savez-vous où il y a un camping par ici ?
ex-kewzay-mwa savay-voo oo eel ya an kompeeng par ee-see

Can we camp here?
On peut camper ici ?
on puh kompay ee-see

How much is it per night?
C'est combien la nuit ?
say komb-yan la nwee

We'd like to stay one night/two nights/a week.
Nous voulons rester une nuit/deux nuits/une semaine.
noo voolon restay ewn nwee/duh nwee/ewn suh-men

Is this drinking water?
Est-ce que c'est de l'eau potable ?
eskuh say duh lo potahbl

Do you sell calor gas?
Vous vendez du butagaz ?
voo vonday dew bewtagaz

Which way to the shops?
Les magasins, s'il vous plaît ?
lay magazan seel voo play

Do you have a map with campsites on it?
Vous avez une carte avec les campings indiqués dessus ?
voo zavay ewn kart avek lay kompeeng andeekay duhsew

CAR ACCIDENTS

He came straight out.
Il est sorti sans regarder
eel ay sortee sōn ruhgarday

He didn't look.
Il n'a pas regardé.
eel na pa ruhgarday

She was going far too fast.
Elle allait vraiment trop vite.
el alay vraymōn tro veet

He went through the red light.
Il a grillé le feu.
eel a greeyay luh fuh

He reversed into me.
Il m'est rentré dedans en reculant.
eel may rōntray duhdōn ōn rekewlōn

She didn't indicate.
Elle n'a pas mis son clignotant.
el na pa mee sōn kleen-yotōn

He was on the wrong side of the road.
Il était du mauvais côté de la route.
eel aytay dew mo-vay ko-tay duh la root

Ok, it was my fault.
Oui, d'accord, c'était ma faute.
wee dakor saytay ma foht

Did you see that?
Vous avez vu ça ?
voo zavay vew sa

Will you be a witness for me?
Vous voulez bien être mon témoin ?
voo voolay b-yān etr mōn taymwān

Can you write down your name and address?
Pouvez-vous écrire votre nom et votre adresse ?
poovay-voo aykreer votr nōm ay votr adress

What's the name of your insurance company?
Quel est le nom de votre compagnie d'assurances ?
kel ay luh nōm duh votr kōmpan-yee dassewrōnss

Do you want to settle this between ourselves?
Vous voulez qu'on arrange ça entre nous ?
voo voolay kōn arōnj sa ōntr noo

Could you call the police?
Pouvez-vous appeler la police ?
poovay-voo aplay la poleess

I'm ok, I'm not hurt.
Ça va, je n'ai rien.
sa va juh nay r-yān

She's been injured.
Elle est blessée.
el ay blessay

Learn to drive!
Apprenez à conduire !
apruhnay a kōndweer

CHEMIST

Is there a chemist open today?
Est-ce qu'il y a une pharmacie ouverte aujourd'hui ?
eskeel ya ewn farma-see oovairt ojoordwee

Is there a chemist open at nights?
Il y a une pharmacie ouverte la nuit ?
eel ya ewn farma-see oovairt la nwee

Have you got something for ...?
Vous avez quelque chose pour ... ?
voo zavay kelkuh shohz poor

Do you have something equivalent to this?
Vous auriez l'équivalent de ça ?
voo zoree-ay laykeevalon̄ duh sa

Can you make up this prescription?
Pouvez-vous me préparer cette ordonnance ?
poovay-voo muh prayparay set ordonon̄ss

YOU'LL SEE

Ne pas avaler.
nuh pa zavalay
Do not swallow.

A prendre avant les repas.
a pron̄dr avon̄ lay ruhpa
Take before meals.

Ne pas laisser à la portée des enfants.
nuh pa lessay a la portay day son̄fon̄
Keep out of reach of children.

CHILDREN AND BABIES

Is there a crèche?
Est-ce qu'il y a une garderie d'enfants ?
eskeel ya ewn garduhree dōnfōn

We need a baby-sitter for tonight.
Il nous faut une baby-sitter pour ce soir.
eel noo fo ewn 'baby-sitter' poor suh swahr

We'll be back at ...
Nous rentrerons à ...
noo rōntruh-rōn a

Can we have a children's portion please?
Peut-on avoir une portion enfant, s'il vous plait ?
puh-tōn avvwahr ewn pors-yōn ōnfōn seel voo play

Two adults and one child to ...
Deux adultes et un enfant pour ...
duh zadewlt ay ān onfōn poor

RESPONSES

Quel âge a-t-il/a-t-elle ?
kel ahj ateel/atel
How old is he/she?

He/she is ... years/months old
Il/elle a ... ans/mois
eel/el a ... ōn/mwa

Isn't he lovely/she lovely!
Comme il est mignon/elle est mignonne
kom eel ay meen-yōn/el ay meen-yon

CINEMA AND THEATRE

Do you have a programme of what's on in town?
Vous auriez un programme des spectacles ?
voo zoree-ay ān program day spektahkl

I'd like to go to the cinema/theatre.
Je voudrais aller au cinéma/au théâtre.
juh voodray alay o seenayma/o tay-ahtr

I want to see a French film/play.
Je voudrais voir un film français/une pièce française.
juh voodray vwahr ān feelm frōnsay/ewn p-yess frōnsez

Can I book two seats for this evening?
Je peux réserver deux places pour ce soir ?
juh puh rayzairvay duh plass poor suh swahr

In the stalls/in the balcony.
A l'orchestre/au balcon.
a lorkestr/o balkōn

How much are tickets for the stalls/for the balcony?
Combien coûtent les tickets à l'orchestre/au balcon ?
kōmb-yān koot lay teekay a lorkestr/o balkōn

I'll pick them up later on.
Je passerai les prendre plus tard.
juh passuhray lay prōndr plew tar

I'll meet you in the foyer.
Je vous retrouverai à l'entrée.
juh voo ruh-troovuhray a lōntray

CLEANING THINGS

Where's the nearest dry cleaner's?
Il y a un pressing près d'ici ?
eel ya an presseeng pray dee-see

Can you clean this/these for me?
Pouvez-vous nettoyer ça ?
poovay-voo netwi-yay sa

When will they be ready?
Ça sera prêt quand ?
sa suhra pray kon

RESPONSES

Cet après-midi.
set apray-meedee
This afternoon.

Demain.
duhman
Tomorrow.

Après-demain.
apray-duhman
The day after tomorrow.

Do you have some clothes pegs?
Vous avez des pinces à linge ?
voo zavay day panss a lanj

Is it ok if I hang my washing out on the roof?
Ça va si j'étends le linge sur le toit ?
sa va see jayton luh lanj sewr luh twa

COMMANDS

To express commands in French take the form of the
verb as given in the dictionary in this book, remove the
endings **-er**, **-ir** or **-re** and then add the following
endings. The left hand column is for the familiar form
'tu' (see *PRONOUNS*):

TU			VOUS
donner	(to give)	**donne**	**donnez**
		don	*donnay*
finir	(to finish)	**finis**	**finissez**
		feenee	*feeneesay*
attendre	(to wait)	**attends**	**attendez**
		aton	*atonday*

Listen!
Ecoutez!
aykootay

Wait for me.
Attendez-moi.
atōnday-mwa

Watch me!
Regardez-moi!
ruhgarday-mwa

Give me that
Donnez-moi ça.
donnay-mwa sa

To tell someone NOT to do something, to give a negative command, put the words **ne ... pas** around the forms as given above:

		TU	**VOUS**
donner	(to give)	**ne donne pas**	**ne donnez pas**
		nuh don pa	*nuh donnay pa*
finir	(to finish)	**ne finis pas**	**ne finissez pas**
		nuh feenee pa	*nuh feeneesay pa*
attendre	(to wait)	**n'attends pas**	**n'attendez pas**
		natoñ pa	*natoñday pa*

Don't speak to him.
Ne lui parlez pas.
nuh lwee parlay pa

Don't wait for me.
Ne m'attendez pas.
nuh matoñday pa

Some irregular forms:

Don't be sad.
Ne sois/soyez pas triste.
nuh swa/swi-yay pa treest

Come here!
Viens/venez ici !
v-yañ/vuhnay ee-see

On signs you might see the form:

> **Ne pas toucher.**
> *nuh pa tooshay*
> Do not touch.

See also SUGGESTIONS.

COMPARISONS

To say that something is, for example, MORE expensive or that something is fastER than something else you use a comparative form of the adjective (or adverb). In French these are all formed by using the word **plus** in front of the adjective or adverb:

fast	**rapide**	*rapeed*
faster	**plus rapide**	*plew rapeed*
expensive	**cher**	*shair*
more expensive	**plus cher**	*plew shair*

Are there any faster trains?
Est-ce qu'il y a des trains plus rapides ?
eskeel ya day trañ plew rapeed

Do you have any bigger ones?
Vous en avez des plus grands ?
voo zoñ avay day plew groñ

Could you speak more slowly please?
Pouvez-vous parler plus lentement, s'il vous plaît ?
poovay-voo parlay plew loñtuhmoñ seel voo play

To say that something is, for example, the MOST expensive or the fastEST, then you use the superlative form of the adjective (or adverb). This is formed by using the words **le plus** in front of the adjective. Of course, if the adjective has to be in the feminine form or in the plural, then you must use **la plus** for feminines and **les plus** for plurals (*see ADJECTIVES*):

fast	**rapide**	*rapeed*
fastest	**le plus rapide**	*luh plew rapeed*
expensive	**cher**	*shair*
most expensive	**le plus cher**	*luh plew shair*

Which is the quickest way to ...?
Quel est le plus court chemin pour aller à ... ?
kel ay luh plew koor shuhmañ poor alay a

The fastest car.
La voiture la plus rapide.
la vwatewr la plew rapeed

Some forms are irregular:

bon	*boñ*	good
mieux	*myuh*	better
le meilleur	*luh may-urr*	best

mauvais	*mo-vay*	bad
pire	*peer*	worse
le pire	*luh peer*	worst

Some more examples:

This one is better THAN that one.
Celui-ci est mieux QUE celui-là.
suhlwee-see ay myuh kuh suhlwee-la

It wasn't AS hard AS I thought.
Ce n'était pas AUSSI difficile QUE je croyais.
suh naytay pa o-see deefeeseel kuh juh krwi-yay

AS fast AS possible.
AUSSI vite QUE possible.
o-see veet kuh poseebl

COMPLAINTS

The ... isn't working.
Le/la ... ne marche pas.
luh/la nuh marsh pa

There's no light in my room.
Il n'y a pas de lumière dans ma chambre.
eel n-ya pa duh lewm-yair dōn ma shōmbr

There's no toilet paper.
Il n'y a pas de papier wc.
eel n-ya pa duh pap-yay vay-say

There's something wrong with this.
Ça ne marche pas bien.
sa nuh marsh pa b-yān

It tastes very peculiar.
Ça a un goût très bizarre.
sa a ān goo tray beezar

It's still not right.
Ça ne va toujours pas.
sa nuh va toojoor pa

I'm not happy about it.
Je n'en suis pas content(e).
juh nōn swee pa kōntōn(t)

I want my money back.
Je voudrais être remboursé(e).
juh voodray etr rōmboorsay

I really think you should accept responsibility.
Je pense que vous devez en accepter la responsabilité.
juh pōnss kuh voo duhvay ōn axeptay la respōn-sabeeleetay

CONVERSIONS

inches
  1 inch = 2.54 centimetres

metres
  1 metre = 39.37 inches or 1.09 yards

kilometres
conversion: kilometres divided by 8, times 5 = miles

kilometres:	1	5	8	10	25	100
miles:	0.6	3.1	5	6.25	15.6	62.5

miles
conversion: miles divided by 5, times 8 = kilometres

miles:	1	3	5	10	20	100
kilometres:	1.6	4.8	8	16	32	160

kilos
conversion: kilos divided by 5, times 11 = pounds

kilos:	1	4	5	10	20	30	40
pounds:	2.2	8.8	11	22	44	66	88

pounds
  1 pound = 0.45 kilos
conversion: pounds divided by 11, times 5 = kilos

litres
  1 litre = approx. 1.75 pints or 0.22 gallons

Centigrade
conversion: C divided by 5, times 9, plus 32 = F

Centigrade:	10	18	25	28	30	34
Fahrenheit:	50	64	77	82	86	93

conversion: F minus 32, divided by 9, times 5 = C

DANCING AND DISCOS

Let's go to a disco.
Allons en boîte.
alōn zōn bwat

Where can we go for ballroom dancing?
Il y a un bal par ici ?
eel ya ān bal par ee-see

Do you want to dance?
Vous voulez danser ?
voo voolay dōnsay

Fancy another dance?
Vous voulez danser encore une fois ?
voo voolay dōnsay ōnkor ewn fwa

I can't do that dance.
Je ne sais pas danser ça.
juh nuh say pa dōnsay sa

Are you here by yourself?
Vous êtes là seul(e) ?
voo zet la surl

Great music.
Super cette musique.
sewpair set mewzeek

I can't hear you.
Je ne vous entends pas.
juh nuh voo zōntōn pa

Let's go to the bar.
Allons au bar.
alōn zo bar

DAYS

Monday	**lundi**	*lāndee*
Tuesday	**mardi**	*mardee*
Wednesday	**mercredi**	*mairkruhdee*
Thursday	**jeudi**	*jurdee*
Friday	**vendredi**	*vōndruhdee*
Saturday	**samedi**	*samdee*
Sunday	**dimanche**	*deemōnsh*

On Monday.
Lundi.
lāndee

On Tuesday evening.
Mardi soir.
mardee swahr

On Saturdays.
Le samedi.
luh samdee

On Saturday nights.
Le samedi soir.
luh samdee swahr

Yesterday.
Hier.
yair

Yesterday morning.
Hier matin.
yair matān

In the mornings.
Le matin.
luh matān

In the evenings.
Le soir.
luh swahr

At nights.
La nuit.
la nwee

This afternoon.
Cet après-midi.
set apray-meedee

The day before yesterday.
Avant-hier.
avo͞nt-yair

Tomorrow.
Demain.
duhma͞n

Tomorrow afternoon.
Demain après-midi.
duhma͞n apray-meedee

The day after tomorrow.
Après-demain.
apray-duhma͞n

Next week.
La semaine prochaine.
la suhmen proshen

DECLINING, SAYING NO

No thank you.
Non merci.
nōn mairsee

That's very kind, but no thanks.
C'est très gentil, mais non merci.
say tray jōntee may nōn mairsee

Thanks all the same though.
Merci quand même.
mairsee kōn mem

I don't really want to.
Ça ne me dit rien.
sa nuh muh dee r-yān

I don't really want one thanks.
Je n'en veux pas vraiment, merci.
juh nōn vuh pa vraymōn mairsee

Not for me/us thanks.
Pas pour moi/nous merci.
pa poor mwa/noo mairsee

Not right now thanks.
Pas maintenant merci.
pa māntuhnōn mairsee

No no, I'm not interested.
Non non, ça ne m'intéresse pas.
nōn nōn sa nuh māntayress pa

I said no!
Je vous ai dit non !
juh voo zay dee nōn

DENTIST

I think I need a filling.
Je crois que j'ai besoin d'un plombage.
juh krwa kuh jay buhzwān dān plōmbahj

I've got/he's got a loose tooth.
J'ai/il a une dent qui bouge.
jay/eel a ewn dōn kee booj

I've got/she's got terrible toothache.
J'ai/elle a une rage de dents terrible.
jay/el a ewn rahj duh dōn taireebl

Can you give me/him an injection?
Pouvez-vous me/lui faire une piqûre ?
poovay-voo muh/lwee fair ewn peekewr

What will it cost?
Ça va coûter combien ?
sa va kootay kōmb-yān

Can you pull it out?
Vous pouvez l'arracher ?
voo poovay larashay

> **Ouvrez grand la bouche.**
> *oovray grōn la boosh*
> Open wide.

> **Ça ne vous fera pas mal.**
> *sa nuh voo fuhra pa mal*
> This won't hurt you.

> **Il faudra l'arracher.**
> *eel fohdra larashay*
> It'll have to come out.

> **Ne mangez pas avant deux heures.**
> *nuh mōnjay pa avōn duh zur*
> Don't eat anything for two hours.

DIRECTIONS

Can you tell me the way to ...?
Pour aller à ..., s'il vous plaît ?
poor alay a seel voo play

I'm looking for Avenue ...
Je cherche l'avenue ...
juh shairsh lavuhnew

Which is the best bus for getting to ...?
Quel bus faut-il prendre pour aller à ...?
kel bewss foteel prondr poor alay a

Could you point it out on the map?
Vous pouvez me montrer sur la carte ?
voo poovay muh mōntray sewr la kart

Which road is it to Aix-en-Provence?
C'est quelle route pour Aix-en-Provence ?
say kel root poor Aix-en-Provence

Is it near ...?
C'est près de ... ?
say pray duh

Excuse me, which street is this?
Excusez-moi, quel est le nom de cette rue ?
ex-kewzay-mwa kel ay le nōm duh set rew

How do I get there?
On y va comment ?
ōn ee va kōmōn

Is it walkable?
On peut y aller à pied ?
ōn puh ee alay a p-yay

Could you just point out the general direction?
Vous pouvez m'indiquer la direction ?
voo poovay mãndeekay la deereks-yōn

RESPONSES

Prenez la première à droite.
pruhnay la pruhm-yair a drwat
Take the first right.

Prenez la deuxième à gauche.
pruhnay la duhz-yem a gohsh
Take the second left.

Aux premiers feux à gauche.
o pruhm-yay fuh a gohsh
Left at the first set of traffic lights.

Allez tout droit.
alay too drwa
Go straight on.

Tout droit après les prochains feux.
too drwa apray lay proshañ fuh
Go straight through the next lights.

Tournez à droite à l'église/à la banque/au musée.
toornay a drwat a laygleez/ala bōñk/o mewzay
Go right at the church/bank/museum.

Traversez le pont.
travairsay luh poñ
Go across the bridge.

Revenez sur vos pas jusqu'à . . .
ruhvuhnay sewr vo pa jewska
Go back this way until . . .

Désolé, je ne suis pas d'ici.
dayzolay juh nuh swee pa dee-see
Sorry, I'm a stranger here.

DISAGREEING WITH PEOPLE

No, that's not right.
Non, ce n'est pas vrai.
non suh nay pa vray

I don't think so.
Je ne pense pas.
juh nuh ponss pa

Oh no.
Non, pas du tout.
non pa dew too

I think you're wrong.
Je pense que vous avez tort.
juh ponss kuh voo zavay tor

He's wrong.
Il a tort.
eel a tor

They're wrong.
Ils ont tort.
eel zon tor

I don't agree with that.
Là je ne suis pas d'accord.
la juh nuh swee pa dakor

Definitely not.
Certainement pas.
sairtenmon pa

No way!
Pas question!
pa kest-yon

DISLIKES

I don't like beer/olives/this hotel.
Je n'aime pas la bière/les olives/cet hôtel.
juh nem pa la b-yair/lay zoleev/set otel

I don't like swimming/sunbathing.
Je n'aime pas me baigner/me faire bronzer.
juh nem pa muh ben-yay/muh fair brõnzay

She doesn't like him.
Il ne lui plaît pas.
eel nuh lwee play pa

I don't like it.
Je n'aime pas ça.
juh nem pa sa

I don't like the look of that.
Ça ne me plaît pas.
sa nuh muh play pa

I can't stand ...
Je ne supporte pas ...
juh nuh sewport pa

I've got a thing about ...
Je n'aime pas ...
juh nem pa

It doesn't taste very nice.
Ça n'a pas très bon goût.
sa na pa tray bõn goo

That's awful.
C'est atroce.
say tatross

It was terrible.
C'était horrible.
saytay orreebl

DOCTOR

Can you call a doctor?
Pouvez-vous appeler un médecin ?
poovay-voo aplay an maydsan

I'm a doctor/a nurse.
Je suis médecin/infirmière.
juh swee maydsan/anfairm-yair

He's had an accident.
Il a eu un accident.
eel a ew an akseedon

I'm/he's/she's ill.
Je suis/il est/elle est malade.
juh swee/eel ay/el ay malad

It's my stomach.
C'est mon ventre.
say mon vontr

It's my back.
C'est mon dos.
say mon do

It's my chest.
C'est ma poitrine.
say ma pwatreen

He fell over/she fell over.
Il est tombé/elle est tombée.
eel ay tombay/el ay tombay

I think it's broken.
Je crois que c'est cassé.
juh krwa kuh say kassay

He's unconscious/she's unconscious.
Il est inconscient/elle est inconsciente.
eel ay ankonsee-on/el ay ankonsee-ont

It hurts here.
Ça fait mal là.
sa fay mal la

It's a very sharp pain.
C'est une douleur très forte.
say tewn doolur tray fort

It just aches.
C'est juste douloureux.
say jewst doolooruh

I've got insurance.
J'ai une assurance médicale.
jay ewn assewrōnss maydeekal

What will it cost?
Ça va coûter combien ?
sa va kootay kōmb-yāñ

RESPONSES

Ça n'a rien de grave.
sa na r-yāñ duh grahv
It's nothing serious.

Vous devez/il doit aller à l'hôpital.
voo duhvay/eel dwa alay a lopeetal
You'll/he'll have to go into hospital.

Il faut vous/l'opérer.
eel fo voo/loopuhray
You'll/he'll/she'll need an operation.

C'est l'appendicite.
say lappōñeeseet
It's appendicitis.

C'est cassé.
say kassay
It's broken.

C'est une crise cardiaque.
say tewn kreez kardee-ak
It's a heart attack.

C'est une intoxication alimentaire.
say tewn āntoxeekass-yōn aleemōntair
It's food poisoning.

Amenez ça chez le pharmacien.
amnay sa shay luh farmass-yān
Take this to a chemist.

DRINKS

What are you drinking?
Qu'est-ce que tu bois/vous buvez ?
keskuh tew bwa/voo bewvay

A cup of coffee please.
Un café, s'il vous plaît.
an kafay seel voo play

Two coffees/teas and a beer.
Deux cafés/thés et une bière.
duh kafay/tay ay ewn b-yair

Two white wines please.
Deux verres de vin blanc, s'il vous plaît.
duh vair duh van blon seel voo play

A carafe of red wine.
Une carafe de vin rouge.
ewn karaf duh van rooj

Dry wine/sweet wine/medium dry wine.
Vin sec/vin doux/vin demi-sec.
van sek/van doo/van duhmee-sek

The same again please.
La même chose, s'il vous plaît.
la mem shohz seel voo play

No ice for me thanks.
Pas de glace pour moi, merci.
pa duh glass poor mwa mairsee

I'd rather have draught beer.
Je préférerais une pression.
juh prayfairuhray ewn press-yon

It's my/your round.
C'est ma/ta/votre tournée.
say ma/ta/votr toornay

DRINKS LIST

bière blonde *b-yair blond* lager
bière brune *b-yair brewn* bitter, dark beer
blanc de blancs *blon duh blon* white wine from white grapes
blanc cassis *blon kasseess* white wine and blackcurrant liqueur
blanc limé *blon leemay* white wine with lemonade
boissons pilotes *bwasson peelot* most common drinks (low priced)
bouteille *bootay* bottle
café crème *kafay krem* white coffee
café frappé *kafay frappay* iced coffee (shaken)
café liégeois *kafay lee-ayj-wa* iced coffee with cream
camomille *kamomeel* camomile tea
cassis *kasseess* blackcurrant drink (often alcoholic)
cidre bouché *seedr booshay* dry cider
cidre doux *seedr doo* sweet cider
citron pressé *seetron pressay* fresh lemon juice
chocolat chaud *shokola sho* hot chocolate
cuvée du patron *kewvay dew patron* house wine
demi *duhmee* small beer
diabolo menthe *dee-abolo mont* mint cordial with lemonade
digestif *deejesteef* liqueur
eau minérale gazeuse *o meenayrahl gazurz* sparkling mineral water
infusion *anfewss-yon* herbal tea
jus d'orange *jew doronj* orange juice
kir *keer* white wine with blackcurrant liqueur
lait grenadine *lay grenadeen* milk with grenadine cordial
menthe à l'eau *mont a lo* mint cordial (often alcoholic)
nectar d'abricot *nektar dabreeko* apricot juice
orange pressée *oronj pressay* freshly squeezed orange juice
panaché *panashay* shandy
pression *press-yon* draught beer
quart de vin *kar duh van* quarter-litre of wine
sirop *seerop* cordial
thé au lait *tay o lay* tea with milk
tilleul *tee-yurl* lime tea
verveine *vairven* verbena tea
vin blanc/rouge *van blon/rooj* white/red wine
vin mousseux *van moossuh* sparkling wine
vin ordinaire *van ordeenair* table wine

DRIVING

(see also CAR ACCIDENTS, GARAGE, RENTALS)

Can I park here?
Je peux me garer ici ?
juh puh muh garay ee-see

Where can I park the car?
Où puis-je garer la voiture ?
oo pwee-juh garay la vwatewr

Where is the nearest petrol station?
Où est la station-essence la plus proche ?
oo ay la stass-yōn-essōnss la plew prosh

Is this the road for …?
C'est bien la route pour …?
say b-yān la root poor

We came by car.
Nous sommes venus en voiture.
noo som vuhnew ōn vwatewr

We're going to drive to …
Nous allons conduire jusqu'à …
noo zalōn kondweer jewska

How long does it take to drive there?
On met combien de temps en voiture pour y aller ?
ōn may kōmb-yān duh tōm ōn vwatewr poor ee alay

It's in the car.
C'est dans la voiture.
say dōn la vwatewr

Let's take my car.
Prenons ma voiture.
pruhnōn ma vwatewr

EMERGENCIES

(*see also THEFT*)

!'m lost.
Je suis perdu(e).
juh swee pairdew

It's broken.
C'est cassé.
say kasay

It's stuck.
C'est coincé.
say kwānsay

Help!
A l'aide, au secours !
a led, o suhkoor

Call the police!
Appelez la police !
aplay la poleess

There's a fire!
Au feu !
o fuh

The tap won't turn off.
Le robinet ne se ferme plus.
luh robeenay nuh suh fairm plew

There's a smell of gas.
Ça sent le gaz.
sa sōn luh gaz

The toilet won't flush.
La chasse ne marche plus.
la shass nuh marsh plew

The ... gives you an electric shock.
Le/la ... envoie des décharges électriques.
luh/la ... õnvwa day daysharj aylektreek

Get a doctor!
Appelez un médecin !
aplay ãn maydsãn

He's had an accident.
Il a eu un accident.
eel a ew ãn axeedõn

It's very urgent.
C'est très urgent.
say tray zewrjõn

I've locked myself out.
Je me suis enfermé(e) dehors.
juh muh swee õnfairmay duh-or

This man is pestering me.
Ce type m'embête.
suh teep mõnbet

Does anyone speak English?
Est-ce que quelqu'un parle anglais ?
eskuh kelkãn parl õnglay

EXPLAINING THINGS

(see also INTENTIONS)

It's necessary to ...
Il faut ...
eel fo

You have to push this button.
Il faut appuyer sur ce bouton.
eel fo apwee-ay sewr suh booton

It's because of the ...
C'est à cause du/de la ...
say ta kohz dew/duh la

You need ...
Il vous faut ...
eel voo fo

I didn't know that.
Je ne savais pas ça.
juh nuh savay pa sa

It wasn't possible to ...
Ce n'était pas possible de ...
suh naytay pa posseebl duh

She didn't understand you, that's why.
C'est parce qu'elle ne vous a pas compris.
say parsskel nuh voo za pa kompree

If you ... then ...
Si vous ... alors ...
see voo ... alor ...

I'll get an interpreter.
Je vais chercher un interprète.
juh vay shairshay an antairpret

FEEL: HOW YOU FEEL

I'm/he's hungry.
J'ai/il a faim.
jay/eel a fañ

I'm/we're thirsty.
J'ai/nous avons soif.
jay/noo zavoñ swaf

I'm/he's tired.
Je suis/il est fatigué.
juh swee/el ay fateegay

I'm/he's bored.
Je m'ennuie/il s'ennuie.
juh mõnwee/eel sõnwee

I'm/they're sleepy.
J'ai /ils ont sommeil.
jay/eel zoñ somay

I feel fine thanks.
Ça va très bien merci.
sa va tray b-yañ mairsee

I feel great!
Je suis en pleine forme.
juh swee zoñ plen form

I feel much better.
Je me sens beaucoup mieux.
juh muh soñ bohkoo m-yuh

He's much better thanks.
Il va bien mieux, merci.
eel va b-yañ m-yuh mairsee

How are you feeling?
Comment ça va ?
komoñ sa va

FLYING

Can you take us to the airport?
Vous pouvez nous emmener à l'aéroport ?
voo poovay noo zonmay a lairopor

Where does the airport bus stop?
Où s'arrête la navette pour l'aéroport ?
oo saret la navet poor lairopor

Is this ok for the airport?
C'est bon pour l'aéroport ?
say bon poor lairopor

I'd like a single/return to . . .
Je voudrais un aller/aller-retour pour . . .
juh voodray an alay/alay-ruhtoor poor

Non-smoking please.
Non fumeurs, s'il vous plaît.
non fewmur seel voo play

Smoking please.
Fumeurs, s'il vous plaît.
fewmur seel voo play

A window seat if possible.
Un siège près de la fenêtre, si possible.
an see-ej pray de la fuhnetr see poseebl

Which gate is it?
C'est quelle porte ?
say kel port

What time is the next flight?
A quelle heure est le prochain vol ?
a kel ur ay luh proshen vol

53

FORBIDDING

You mustn't ...
Il ne faut pas ...
eel nuh fo pa

You shouldn't do that.
Il ne faut pas faire ça.
eel nuh fo pa fair sa

Don't do that.
Ne faites pas ça.
nuh fet pa sa

Don't do anything until I say so.
Ne faites rien avant que je vous le dise
nuh fet r-yān avōn kuh juh voo luh deez

He's not to ...
Il ne doit pas ...
eel nuh dwa pa

That's not allowed.
Ce n'est pas permis.
suh nay pa pairmee

There's no way you can borrow it.
Vous ne pouvez absolument pas l'emprunter.
voo nuh poovay absolewmōn pa lōmprāntay

Stop that right now!
Arrêtez ça tout de suite.
aretay sa too duh sweet

Interdit de ...	**Défense de ...**
No ...	... forbidden
Ne pas ...	
Do not ...	

54

FRANCE

With an area of 550,000 square kilometres and a population of approximately 56 million (as compared with the UK's 244,000 square kilometres and 56 million population) France is the largest country in Western Europe.

The capital city, Paris, with a population of just over 2 million, is divided into 20 **arrondissements** or administrative districts. In spite of various efforts at decentralization, Paris remains a central influence at economical, political and social levels. The three major cities after Paris are Marseille, Lyon and Bordeaux.

France has been a republic since 1792 and has both a president and a prime minister.

The country is divided into 22 regions which are again divided into **départements** - there are 95 of these, including Corsica.

France is a country of widely differing landscapes. Low-lying country in the north and west contrasts with the mountainous regions of the south and east. Mont Perdu in the Pyrenees is 3,352 metres high and, in the Alps, Mont-Blanc (Europe's highest mountain) rises to 4,807 metres. The four major rivers are the Loire, the Seine, the Garonne and the Rhône.

The climate is influenced by both Atlantic and Mediterranean factors. In the north and north west the winters are fairly mild. In the east the climate is harsher, more continental. The south has mild winters and dry, hot summers although the cooling Mistral wind sweeps down the Rhône valley.

Major national holidays are the 14th of July (le Quatorze Juillet) − the anniversary of the storming of the Bastille during the French Revolution − and the 15th of August (le Quinze Août).

FUTURE

To talk about what is going to happen in the future you can very often use the present tense (*see PRESENT*). English works in a similar way, for example:

Our train leaves at 11.00 tomorrow.
Notre train part demain à onze heures.
notr trā̄n par duhmā̄n a ō̄nz ur

I'm going home next week.
Je rentre à la maison la semaine prochaine.
juh rō̄ntr a la mezzō̄n la suhmen proshen

French often uses the present tense where English uses the future:

I'll be right back.
Je reviens tout de suite.
juh ruhv~yā̄n toot duh sweet

The actual future tense in French, used to say 'I WILL, you WILL' etc is formed by making the following changes to the verbs as given in the dictionary section:

donner (to give) − I *etc* will give

je donnerai *donnuhray*	**nous donnerons** *donnuhrō̄n*
tu donneras *donnuhra*	**vous donnerez** *donnuhray*
il/elle donnera *donnuhra*	**ils/elles donneront** *donnuhrō̄n*

finir (to finish) − I *etc* will finish

je finirai *feeneeray*	**nous finirons** *feeneerō̄n*
tu finiras *feeneera*	**vous finirez** *feeneeray*
il/elle finira *feeneera*	**ils/elles finiront** *feeneerō̄n*

attendre (to wait) − I *etc* will wait

j'attendrai *atōndray*	**nous attendrons** *atōndrōn*
tu attendras *atōndra*	**vous attendrez** *atōndray*
il/elle attendra *atōndra*	**ils/elles attendront** *atōndrōn*

Some common irregular verbs:

être (to be) − I *etc* will be

je serai *suhray*	**nous serons** *suhrōn*
tu seras *suhra*	**vous serez** *suhray*
il/elle sera *suhra*	**ils/elles seront** *suhrōn*

avoir (to have) − I *etc* will have

j'aurai *joray*	**nous aurons** *orōn*
tu auras *ora*	**vous aurez** *oray*
il/elle aura *ora*	**ils/elles auront** *orōn*

aller (to go) − I *etc* will go

j'irai *jeeray*	**nous irons** *eerōn*
tu iras *eera*	**vous irez** *eeray*
il/elle ira *eera*	**ils/elles iront** *eerōn*

venir (to come) − I *etc* will come

je viendrai *v-yāndray*	**nous viendrons** *v-yāndrōn*
tu viendras *v-yāndra*	**vous viendrez** *v-yāndray*
il/elle viendra *v-yāndra*	**ils/elles viendront** *v-yāndrōn*

GARAGES

(see also DRIVING)

30 litres of 4-star/2-star please.
30 litres de super/normal, s'il vous plaît.
tront leetr duh sewpair/normahl seel voo play

Could you fill it up?
Vous pouvez faire le plein ?
voo poovay fair luh plan

1 litre of oil.
Un litre d'huile.
an leetr dweel

Do you do repairs?
Vous faites les réparations ?
voo fet lay rayparass-yon

Could you have a look at the front brakes/rear brakes?
Vous pouvez vérifier les freins avant/les freins arrière ?
voo poovay vayreefee-ay lay fran zavon/lay fran zaree-air

There's something wrong with the clutch.
Il y a quelque chose qui ne va pas avec l'embrayage.
eel ya kelkuh shohz kee nuh va pa avek lombray-yahj

It's losing water.
Elle perd de l'eau.
el pair duh lo

It's overheating.
Le moteur chauffe.
luh motur shohf

It keeps cutting out.
Elle n'arrête pas de caler.
el naret pa duh kalay

It takes a long time to start.
Elle a du mal à démarrer.
el a dew mal a daymaray

The steering is very slack.
La direction est très lâche.
la deereks-yoñ ay tray lahsh

The door won't lock.
La porte ne ferme plus à clef.
la port nuh fairm plew a klay

The lights are faulty.
Les phares ne marchent pas bien.
lay far nuh marsh pa b-yañ

I need a new indicator bulb.
Il me faut une ampoule pour le clignotant.
eel muh fo tewn oñpool poor luh kleen-yotoñ

Can you do it now?
Vous pouvez le faire maintenant ?
voo poovay luh fair mañtuhnoñ

Can you do it today?
Vous pouvez le faire aujourd'hui ?
voo poovay luh fair ojoordwee

When can I pick it up?
Je peux la prendre quand ?
juh puh la proñdr koñ

HAIRDRESSER

Just a trim please.
Juste pour rafraîchir la coupe, s'il vous plaît.
jewst poor rafresheer la koop seel voo play

Could you take 2 inches off all round?
Vous pouvez les raccourcir de cinq centimètres ?
voo poovay rakoorseer duh sănk sŏnteemetr

Could you tidy up the ends?
Vous pouvez couper les pointes ?
voo poovay koopay lay pwăn

Not too short.
Pas trop court.
pa tro koor

Could you thin it out a bit?
Vous pouvez désépaissir un peu ?
voo poovay dayzaypesseer ăn puh

On top.
Sur le dessus.
sewr luh duhsew

At the sides.
Sur les côtés.
sewr lay kohtay

I'd like it a lot shorter.
Je voudrais les avoir beaucoup plus courts.
juh voodray lay zavwahr bohkoo plew koor

Up to about here.
A peu près jusque là.
a puh pray jewskuh la

Just over the ears.
Sur les oreilles.
sewr lay zoray

A shampoo and set please.
Un shampoing et une mise en plis, s'il vous plaît.
an shompwan ay ewn mee zon plee seel voo play

Can you put highlights in?
Vous pouvez me faire des mèches ?
voo poovay muh fair day mesh

Can you do the roots?
Vous pouvez refaire les racines ?
voo poovay ruhfair lay rasseen

Can you give me a perm?
Vous pouvez me faire une permanente ?
voo poovay muh fair ewn pairmanont

Tight curls/loose curls.
Boucles serrées/une mini-vague.
bookl sairray/ewn meenee-vag

RESPONSES

Vous voulez de l'après-shampoing ?
voo voolay duh lapray-shompwan
Would you like conditioner?

Un brushing ?
an brusheeng
A blow dry?

61

HELLO – GOODBYE

Hello.
Bonjour; *(in the evening)* bonsoir.
bōnjoor; bōnswahr

Hi there.
Salut.
salew

Goodbye.
Au revoir.
o-ruhvwahr

Cheerio.
Tchao.
chow

See you later.
A plus tard.
a plew tar

Good morning/good afternoon.
Bonjour.
bōnjoor

Good evening.
Bonsoir.
bōnswahr

Good night.
Bonne nuit.
bon nwee

Pleased to meet you.
Enchanté.
ōnshōntay

It was nice meeting you.
J'ai été très content(e) de vous rencontrer.
jay aytay tray kōntōn(t) duh voo rōnkōntray

HITCH-HIKING

Are you going to …?
Vous allez à … ?
voo zalay a

Are you going anywhere near …?
Est-ce que vous allez près de … ?
eskuh voo zalay pray duh

Can you give me/us a lift?
Vous pouvez me/nous prendre ?
voo poovay muh/noo prondr

We've been standing here for two hours.
Ça fait deux heures qu'on attend.
sa fay duh zur kon aton

Do you have room for four people?
Vous avez de la place pour quatre personnes ?
voo zavay duh la plass poor katr pairson

Can you drop us off here/at the next services?
Vous pouvez nous laisser là/à la prochaine station-service ?
voo poovay noo lessay la/a la proshen stass-yon-sairveess

That's very kind of you.
C'est très gentil de votre part.
say tray jontee duh votr par

RESPONSES

Où allez-vous ?
oo alay-voo
Where are you going?

Je ne vais pas plus loin que …
juh nuh vay pa plew lwan kuh
I'm only going as far as …

63

HOSPITAL

(see also DOCTOR)

Can you take us to the hospital?
Pouvez-vous nous emmener à l'hôpital ?
poovay-voo noo zōmnay a lopeetal

To the casualty department.
Au service des urgences.
o sairveess day zewrjōnss

To the maternity unit.
A la maternité.
a la matairneetay

Which ward is he/she in?
Il/elle est dans quel service ?
eel/el ay dōn kel sairveess

How is he/she doing?
Comment va-t-il/elle?
kōmōn vateel/el

RESPONSES

Mieux/pas très bien.
m-yuh/pa tray b-yān
Better/not very well.

When are visiting hours?
Quand sont les heures de visite ?
kōn sōn lay zur duh veezeet

How long will I/he have to stay in for?
Je dois/il doit rester combien de temps ?
juh dwa/eel dwa restay kōmb-yān duh tōm

Is treatment covered by this insurance?
Le traitement est couvert par l'assurance médicale?
luh tretmōn ay koovair par lassewrōnss maydeekal

HOTELS

(see also SELF-CATERING)

Do you have a room for one night?
Vous avez une chambre pour une nuit ?
voo zavay ewn shōmbr poor ewn nwee

For two nights/for a week.
Pour deux nuits/pour une semaine.
poor duh nwee/poor ewn suhmen

Do you have a single/double room?
Vous avez une chambre pour une personne/deux personnes ?
voo zavay ewn shōmbr poor ewn pairson/duh pairson

For two people/for two adults and one child.
Pour deux personnes/pour deux adultes et un enfant.
poor duh pairson/poor duh zadewlt ay ān ōnfōn

I have a reservation.
J'ai réservé.
jay rayzairvay

How much is it per night?
C'est combien la nuit ?
say kōmb-yān la nwee

Could you write the cost down?
Pouvez-vous écrire le prix ?
poovay-voo aykreer luh pree

We'd like a room with two single beds.
Nous voulons une chambre avec deux lits à une place.
noo voolōn ewn shōmbr avek duh lee a ewn plass

We'd like a room with a double bed.
Nous voulons une chambre avec un grand lit.
noo voolōn ewn shōmbr avek ān grōn lee

Can we see the room?
On peut voir la chambre ?
ōn puh vwahr la shōmbr

RESPONSES

C'est à quel nom ?
say ta kel nōm
Your name please?

Vous voulez bien signer ici ?
voo voolay b-yān seen-yay ee-see
Could you sign here?

Je peux voir votre passeport ?
juh puh vwahr votr passpor
Can I see your passport?

Comment payez-vous ?
kōmōn pay-ay-voo
How will you be paying?

By credit card/cash.
Par carte/en espèces.
par kart/ōn esspess

Can I have the bill for room 212 please?
Je peux avoir la note pour la chambre 212, s'il vous plaît ?
juh puh avwahr la not poor la shōmbr duh-sōn-dooz seel voo play

I'd like to stay another night.
Je voudrais rester une nuit de plus.
juh voodray restay ewn nwee duh plew

Another two nights.
Deux nuits de plus.
duh nwee duh plew

IDIOMS

Il tombe des cordes.
eel tōmb day kord
It's raining cats and dogs.

Ça coûte les yeux de la tête.
sa koot lay z-yuh de la tet
It costs a fortune.

J'ai dormi comme un loir.
jay dormee kom ān lwa
I slept like log.

C'est pas demain la veille.
say pa duhmān la vay
It's not going to happen that quickly.

Il ne manquerait plus que ça.
eel nuh mōnkuhray plew kuh sa
That's all we'd need.

Elle m'a tapé dans l'œil.
el ma tapay dōn luh-ee
She caught my eye.

Tu as un poil dans la main.
tew a ān pwal dōn la mān
You're a lazy so-and-so.

Pour des prunes.
poor day prewn
For nothing.

Il est rond comme une queue de pelle.
eel ay rōn kom ewn kuh duh pel
He's as drunk as a newt.

Elle fume comme un pompier.
el fewm kom ān pōmp-yay
She smokes like a chimney.

INTENTIONS

What are you going to do?
Qu'est-ce que vous allez faire ?
keskuh voo zalay fair

I'll be back soon.
Je reviens tout de suite.
juh ruhv-yañ too duh sweet

I'll bring it back this afternoon/tomorrow.
Je le/la ramène cet après-midi/demain.
juh luh/la ramen set apray-meedee/duhmañ

I'll go to the bank and then come back with the money.
Je vais à la banque et je reviens avec l'argent.
juh vay a la boñk ay juh ruhv-yañ avek larjoñ

I'll give it to him for you.
Je le lui donnerai pour vous.
juh luh lwee donnuhray poor voo

I'll leave this here as a deposit.
Je le laisse ici en guise d'accompte.
juh luh less ee-see oñ geez dakoñt

I'm coming back next week.
Je reviens la semaine prochaine.
juh ruhv-yañ la suhmen proshen

I'll do something about it, I promise.
Je m'en occuperai, je vous le promets.
juh moñ nokewpuhray juh voo luh promay

I'll go and get . . .
Je vais chercher . . .
juh vay shairshay

68

INVITING PEOPLE

Would you like to ...?
Vous voulez ... ?
voo voolay

Would you like to come with us?
Vous voulez venir avec nous?
voo voolay vuhneer avek noo

Would you like to have a drink?
Vous voulez prendre un verre ?
voo voolay prondr an vair

Would you like to come out this evening?
Vous voulez sortir ce soir ?
voo voolay sorteer suh swahr

What are you doing tonight?
Qu'est-ce que vous faites ce soir ?
keskuh voo fet suh swahr

How about a meal this evening?
Ça vous dit d'aller au restaurant ce soir ?
sa voo dee dalay o restoron suh swahr

We'd like to invite you out.
Nous aimerions vous inviter.
noo zemuhree-on voo zanveetay

Thanks for the invitation, but ...
Merci pour l'invitation, mais ...
mairsee poor lanveetass-yon may

LIKES

I like this wine.
J'aime ce vin.
jem suh vãn

I like swimming/sunbathing.
J'aime bien nager/me faire bronzer.
jem b-yãn nahjay/muh fair brõnzay

She likes him.
Elle l'aime bien.
el lem b-yãn

I like it.
Ça me plaît.
sa muh play

I like it here.
Ça me plaît ici.
sa muh play ee-see

Do you like it?
Ça vous plaît ?
sa voo play

I love you.
Je t'aime.
juh tem

I love this beer/these colours.
J'aime cette bière/ces couleurs.
jem set b-yair/say koolur

It's beautiful. (food etc)
C'est délicieux.
say dayleess-yuh

It was fantastic.
C'était extra.
saytay extra

MAP

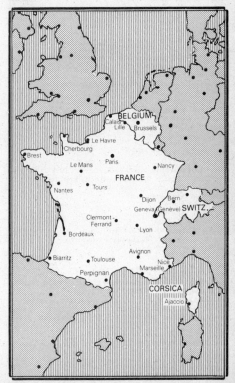

MENU READER

agneau *an-yo* lamb
ail *i* garlic
ailloli *i-olee* garlic mayonnaise
à l'ancienne *a lõnsee-en* traditional style
à la provençale *a la provõnsahl* with tomatoes, garlic and herbs
ananas *anana* pineapple
andouillette *õndwee-yet* small strong-tasting sausage
anguille *õn-gwee* eel
à point *a pwãn* medium
artichaut *arteesho* artichoke
aspic de volaille *aspeek duh voli* chicken in aspic
assiette anglaise *assee-yet õnglez* selection of cold meats
au choix *o shwa* choice of

baguette *baget* French stick
bar *bar* bass
bavette à l'échalote *bavet a layshalot* grilled beef with shallots
béchamel *bayshamel* béchamel sauce (milk, butter and flour)
beignet *ben-yay* fritter, doughnut
betterave *betrahv* beetroot
beurre *bur* butter
bien cuit *b-yãn kwee* well done
bifteck *beeftek* steak
bisque de homard *beesk duh omar* lobster bisque
blanquette de veau *blõnket duh vo* veal stew
bleu *bluh* very rare
bleu d'Auvergne *bluh dovairn* strong blue cheese from Auvergne
bœuf *burf* beef
bœuf bourguignon *burf boorgeen-yon* beef cooked in red wine
bœuf en daube *burf õn dohb* beef casserole
bouchée à la reine *booshay a la ren* vol au vent
boudin *boodãn* black pudding
bouillabaisse *boo-yabess* fish soup from the the south of France
bouillon *boo-yõn* broth
brandade de morue *brõndahd duh morew* cod in cream and garlic
brioche *bree-osh* round bun
brochette *broshet* kebab
brugnon *brewn-yõn* nectarine

calmar *kalmar* squid
canard *kanar* duck
canard laqué *kanar lakay* Peking duck
cantal *kŏntal* hard cheese from Auvergne
cari *karee* curry
carottes Vichy *karot veeshee* boiled carrots in butter and parsley
carte *kart* menu
casse-croûte *kass-kroot* snacks
cassis *kasseess* blackcurrant
cassoulet *kassoolay* casserole of pork, sausages and beans
céleri rémoulade *selree ruhmoolahd* celeriac in mustard dressing
cerise *suhreez* cherry
cervelle *sairvel* brains
champignon de Paris *shŏmpeen-yŏn duh paree* champignon (cultivated mushroom)
champignons à la grecque *shŏmpeen-yŏn a la grek* mushrooms in olive oil and herbs
chantilly *shŏntee-yee* whipped cream
chausson aux pommes *shosson o pom* apple turnover
charlotte *sharlot* cake made of thick custard, fruits and biscuits
chèvre *shevr* goat's cheese
chiffonnade d'oseille *sheefonahd dozay* seasoned sorrel cooked in butter
chocolatine *shokolateen* chocolate-filled bun
chou *shoo* cabbage
chou à la crème *shoo a la krem* cream puff
choucroute *shookroot* sauerkraut with sausages etc
chou-fleur *shooflur* cauliflower
choux de Bruxelles *shoo duh brewksel* Brussels sprouts
citron *seetrŏn* lemon
civet de lièvre *seevay duh lee-evr* jugged hare
comté *kŏmtay* hard cheese from the Jura area
concombre *kŏnkombr* cucumber
confit d'oie *kŏnfee dwa* goose preserved in fat
coq au vin *kok o văn* chicken in red wine
coquilles Saint-Jacques *kokee săn jak* scallops
côte de porc *koht duh por* pork chop
coulis *koolee* fruity or savoury sauce
coulommiers *koolomee-ay* rich cheese like Camembert

73

couscous *kooskoos* semolina with meat, vegetables and a hot spicy sauce

couvert *koovair* cover charge

crème anglaise *krem ōnglez* custard

crème pâtissière *krem pateess-yair* rich and creamy custard

crème renversée *krem rōnvairsay* crème caramel

crêpe *krep* pancake

cresson *kressōn* watercress

crevette *krevet* prawn

croque-Madame *krok-madahm* toasted cheese and ham sandwich with a fried egg on top

croque-Monsieur *krok-muh-sewr* toasted cheese sandwich with ham

crottin de Chavignol *krotān duh shaveen-yol* goat's cheese (bite-sized)

cru *krew* raw

crudités *krewdeetay* selection of salads, chopped raw vegetables

cuisses de grenouille *kweess duh gruh-nwee* frogs' legs

daurade *dorahd* gilt-head (fish)

déjeuner *dayjurnay* lunch

dinde *dānd* turkey

dîner *deenay* dinner

échalote *ayshalot* shallot

écrevisse *aykruhveess* freshwater crayfish

émincé de veau *aymānssay duh vo* finely cut veal in a cream sauce

endives au jambon *ōndeev o jōnbōn* endives with ham cooked in the oven

entrecôte *ōntr-koht* rib steak

entrecôte maître d'hôtel *ōntr-koht metr dotel* rib steak with butter and parsley

entrée *ōntray* starter

épaule d'agneau farcie *aypohl dan-yo farsee* stuffed shoulder of lamb

escalope panée *eskalop panay* breaded escalope

escargots *eskargo* snails

estouffade de bœuf *estoofahd duh burf* beef casserole

faisan *fezōn* pheasant

farci *farsee* stuffed
fenouil *fen-wee* fennel
filet *feelay* fillet
financière *feenōnss-yair* rich sauce, served with sweetbreads or dumplings
flageolets *flajolay* kidney beans
flambé *flōmbay* flambé, flamed with alcohol
flan *flōn* custard tart, crème caramel
foie gras *fwa gra* goose liver preserved in fat
fondue bourguignonne *fōndew boorgeen-yōn* meat fondue
foies de volaille *fwa duh vol-ī* chicken livers
fondue savoyarde *fōndew sav-wi-ard* cheese and white wine fondue
fraise *frez* strawberry
framboise *frōmbwahz* raspberry
frangipane *frōnjeepan* almond pastry
frit *free* deep fried
frites *freet* chips, French fries
fromage *fromahj* cheese
fromage blanc *fromahj blōn* creamy cottage cheese
fruits de mer *frwee duh mair* seafood

garni *garnee* with potatoes and vegetables
gibelotte de lapin *jeeblot duh lapān* rabbit stewed in white wine
gibier *jeeb-yay* game
gigot d'agneau *jeego dan-yo* leg of lamb
girolle *jeerol* chanterelle (mushroom)
glace *glass* ice cream
gratin *gratān* baked cheese dish
gratin dauphinois *gratān dofeenwa* potatoes with grated cheese cooked in the oven
gratinée *grateenay* baked onion soup
groseille rouge *grosī rooj* redcurrant

hareng saur *arōn sor* smoked herring
haricots *areeko* beans
haricot de mouton *areeko duh mootōn* mutton stew with beans
homard *omar* lobster
homard à l'américaine *omar a lamayreeken* lobster with tomatoes and white wine

huîtres *weetr* oysters

jambon *jōnbōn* ham
jarret de veau *jarray duh vo* shin of veal
julienne *jewlee-en* soup with chopped vegetables

langue de bœuf *lōng duh burf* ox tongue
lapin *lapān* rabbit
lapin de garenne *lapān duh garren* wild rabbit
lard *lar* bacon
légumes *laygewm* vegetables
lentilles *lōnteel* lentils
lièvre *lee-evr* hare
livarot *leevaro* strong-tasting cheese from the north of France
loup au fenouil *loo po fuhnwee* bass with fennel

macédoine de légumes *massaydwan duh laygewm* mixed chopped vegetables
mâche *mash* lamb's lettuce
magret de canard *magray duh kanar* duck breast
marron *marrōn* chestnut
menthe *mōnt* peppermint
menu gastronomique *muhnew gastronomeek* gourmet menu
moules marinière *mool mareen-yair* mussels in white wine
mouton *mootōn* mutton
munster *manstair* strong cheese from eastern France
myrtille *meertee* bilberry

nature *natewr* plain
navarin *navarān* mutton stew with vegetables
navet *navay* turnip
noisette *nwazet* hazelnut
noix *nwa* walnut

œuf dur *urf dewr* hard boiled egg
œuf mollet *urf molay* soft boiled egg
œufs à la neige *ur a la nej* floating islands, whipped egg whites on custard
œufs brouillés *ur broo-yay* scrambled eggs
œuf sur le plat *urf sewr luh pla* fried egg
oie *wa* goose
oignon *on-yōn* onion

omelette aux fines herbes *omlet o feen zairb* omelette with chives

orange givrée *oronj jeevray* orange sorbet served in a hollowed-out orange

oseille *ozay* sorrel

oursin *oorsan* sea urchin

pain *pan* bread

palette de porc *palet duh por* shoulder of pork

pamplemousse *pompl-mooss* grapefruit

pané *panay* breaded

pâtes *paht* pasta

paupiettes de veau *popee-yet duh vo* rolled up slices of veal with a filling

pêche *pesh* peach

petit déjeuner *puhtee dayjurnay* breakfast

petite friture *puhteet freetewr* whitebait

petits fours *puhtee foor* small fancy pastries

petits pois *puhtee pwa* green peas

petit suisse *puhtee swess* light white cream cheese

piperade *peepuhrahd* Basque egg dish with tomatoes and peppers

plat du jour *pla dew joor* today's special

plateau de fromages *plato duh fromahj* cheese board

poire *pwahr* pear

poireau *pwahro* leek

poire belle Hélène *pwahr bel aylen* pear in chocolate sauce

poisson *pwasson* fish

poivron *pwahvron* pepper (vegetable)

pomme *pom* apple

pomme de terre *pom duh tair* potato

pommes Dauphine *pom dofeen* potato fritters

pommes paille *pom pi* finely cut French fries

pommes vapeur *pom vapur* boiled potatoes

pot au feu *po toh fuh* beef and vegetable hot pot

potage *potahj* soup

potage velouté *potahj vuhlootay* creamy soup

potée *potay* vegetable and meat stew

poulet à l'estragon *poolay a lestragon* chicken in tarragon sauce

poulet basquaise *poolay baskez* chicken with bacon, tomatoes and peppers

poulet chasseur *poolay shassur* chicken with mushrooms and white wine

prune *prewn* plum

purée *pewray* mashed potatoes

quenelle *kuhnel* dumpling

raclette *raklet* Swiss dish of melted cheese

ragoût *ragoo* stew

raisin *rezan* grapes

reblochon *ruh-bloshon* strong cheese from Savoy

rigotte *reegot* bite-sized goat's cheese from the Lyons area

rillettes *ree-yet* potted pork or goose meat

ris de veau *ree duh vo* veal sweetbread

rissole *reesohl* meat pie

riz *ree* rice

rognons *ron-yon* kidneys

roquefort *rokfor* blue ewe's cheese

rôti *rohtee* joint, roast

rouget *roojay* red mullet

rouille *roo-yuh* sauce served with fish soup

saignant *sen-yon* rare

saint-marcellin *san marsuhlan* very strong cheese

salade niçoise *salahd neess-wahz* salad with olives, tomatoes and anchovies

salsifis *salseefee* oyster plant, salsify

sauce hollandaise *sohss olondez* rich sauce served with fish

sauce matelote *sohss matlot* wine sauce

sauce Mornay *sohss mornay* béchamel sauce with cheese

sauce poulette *sohss poolet* sauce with mushrooms, egg yolks and wine

saucisse *sohseess* sausage

saucisse de Strasbourg *sohseess duh strasboorg* beef sausage

saucisson *sohseeson* salami-type sausage

saumon *sohmon* salmon

seiche *sesh* cuttlefish

sel *sel* salt

selon arrivage *suhlon arreevahj* depending on availability

service (non) compris *sairvees (non) kompree* service (not) included

soupe à l'oignon *soop a lon-yon* onion soup

soupe au pistou *soop o peestoo* thick vegetable soup with basil
soupe de poissons *soop duh pwasson* fish soup
steak au poivre *stayk o pwahvr* pepper steak
steak frites *stayk freet* steak and chips
steak hâché *stayk ashay* minced meat steak, 100% beefburger
steak tartare *stayk tartar* raw minced beef with seasoning and a raw egg on top
sucre *sewkr* sugar

tarte *tart* tart, pie
tarte Tatin *tart tatan* baked apple dish
tartine *tarteen* slice of bread and butter
terrine *terreen* coarse pâté
tête de veau *tet duh vo* veal's brawn in aspic
thon *ton* tuna fish
tomates farcies *tomaht farsee* stuffed tomatoes
tome de Savoie *tohm duh savva* white cheese from Savoy
tournedos *toornuhdo* round fillet steak
tourte *toort* pie
tripes à la mode de Caen *treep a la mod duh kon* tripe with a spicy tomato sauce
truite au bleu *trweet o bluh* poached trout
truite meunière *trweet muhn-yair* fried trout

vacherin *vashran* strong cheese from the Jura area
vacherin glacé *vashran glasay* ice cream meringue
veau *vo* veal
velouté *vuhlootay* creamy soup
viande *v-yond* meat
volaille *voli* poultry

MONEY

(see also *BANKS*)

How much is it?
C'est combien ?
say kōmb-yān

How much is this?
Ça coûte combien, ça ?
sa koot kōmb-yān sa

What does that come to?
Ça fait combien ?
sa fay kōmb-yān

Could you write that down?
Vous pouvez l'écrire ?
voo poovay laykreer

Can I use this? (credit card)
Je peux payer avec ça ?
juh puh pay-ay avek sa

Can I have the bill please?
Je peux avoir la note, s'il vous plaît?
juh puh avwahr la not seel voo play

No I'll pay
Non, c'est moi qui paie.
nōn say mwa kee pay

Can we pay together?
On peut payer ensemble ?
ōn puh pay-ay ōnsōmbl

Can we pay separately?
On peut payer séparément ?
ōn puh pay-ay sayparaymōn

Can I pay straight away?
Je peux payer tout de suite ?
juh puh pay-ay too duh sweet

Keep the change.
Gardez la monnaie.
garday la monnay

Call it 300.
Arrondissez à 300 francs.
arondeesay a trwa-son fron

That's not right surely.
Je pense qu'il y a une erreur.
juh ponss keel ya ewn air-rur

That's too expensive.
C'est trop cher.
say tro shair

Can you give me coins for this?
Vous pouvez me faire la monnaie ?
voo poovay muh fair la monnay

I'm broke.
Je suis fauché(e).
juh swee fohshay

He's loaded.
Il est plein aux as.
eel ay plan o zas

Can I have a refund?
Je peux être remboursé(e) ?
juh puh etr romboorsay

Excuse me, do you have any change?
Excusez-moi, avez-vous de la monnaie ?
ex-kewzay-mwa avay-voo duh la monnay

MONTHS

January	janvier	*jōnvee-ay*
February	février	*fayvree-ay*
March	mars	*marss*
April	avril	*avreel*
May	mai	*may*
June	juin	*jwān*
July	juillet	*jwee-ay*
August	août	*oot*
September	septembre	*septōmbr*
October	octobre	*oktobr*
November	novembre	*novōmbr*
December	décembre	*daysōmbr*

This month.
Ce mois-ci.
suh mwa-see

Next month/last month.
Le mois prochain/le mois dernier.
luh mwa proshān/luh mwa dairn-yay

In March/August.
En mars/en août.
ōn marss/ōn oot

In the summer months.
Les mois d'été.
lay mwa daytay

During the winter months.
Les mois d'hiver.
lay mwa deevair

NECESSITY, OBLIGATION

Do I have to ...?
Je dois ... ?
juh dwa

We have to go now.
Il faut partir maintenant.
eel fo parteer māntuhnōn

Is it necessary to pay in advance?
Il faut payer en avance ?
eel fo pay-ay ōn avōnss

That's not necessary.
Ça n'est pas nécessaire.
sa nay pa naysessair

When do we have to be back by?
A quelle heure faut-il être rentré ?
a kel ur fohteel etr rōntray

You must ...
Vous devez ...
voo duhvay

You must not ...
Vous ne devez pas ...
voo nuh duhvay pa

It must be ready tomorrow.
Ça doit être prêt demain
sa dwa tetr pray duhmān

You shouldn't do that.
Vous ne devriez pas faire ça.
voo nuh duhvree-ay pa fair sa

NEGATIVES

To express a negative in French, to say 'I DON'T know', 'it's NOT here' etc, you use the words **ne ... pas** placed around the verb:

I know.	I don't know.
Je sais.	**Je ne sais pas.**
juh say	*juh nuh say pa*
He knows.	He doesn't know.
Il sait.	**Il ne sait pas.**
eel say	*eel nuh say pa*
She's here.	She's not here.
Elle est là.	**Elle n'est pas là.**
el ay la	*el nay pa la*

If the verb is in the past tense (*see PAST*) the **ne ... pas** is used as follows:

I bought it.	I didn't buy it.
Je l'ai acheté.	**Je ne l'ai pas acheté.**
juh lay ash-tay	*juh nuh lay pa ash-tay*

The following work in the same way as **ne ... pas**:

ne ... jamais	**ne ... plus**	**ne ... rien**
nuh ... jamay	*nuh ... plew*	*nuh ... r-yān*
never	no more	nothing

I've never eaten it.
Je n'en ai jamais mangé.
juh nōn ay jamay mōnjay

He doesn't want to any more.
Il ne veut plus.
eel nuh vuh plew

84

I didn't say anything (I said nothing).
Je n'ai rien dit.
juh nay r-yān dee

If there is no verb, just use **pas**:

Not him!
Pas lui !
pa lwee

Not now.
Pas maintenant.
pa māntuhnōn

Sometimes the **ne** can be left out:

It's not true.
C'est pas vrai.
say pa vray

To say **no** with nouns (no sugar, no cigarettes) use **pas de**:

No sugar for me thanks.
Pas de sucre pour moi merci.
pas de sookr poor mwah mairsee

There is no (isn't any) soap.
Il n'y a pas de savon.
eel n-ya pa duh sa-von

NUMBERS

0	zéro	*zayro*
1	un	*ān*
2	deux	*duh*
3	trois	*trwa*
4	quatre	*katr*
5	cinq	*sānk*
6	six	*seess*
7	sept	*set*
8	huit	*weet*
9	neuf	*nuhf*
10	dix	*deess*
11	onze	*ōnz*
12	douze	*dooz*
13	treize	*trez*
14	quatorze	*katorz*
15	quinze	*kānz*
16	seize	*sez*
17	dix-sept	*deeset*
18	dix-huit	*deez-weet*
19	dix-neuf	*deez-nuhf*
20	vingt	*vān*
21	vingt et un	*vāntay-ān*
22	vingt-deux	*vān-duh*
30	trente	*trōnt*
35	trente-cinq	*trōnt-sānk*
40	quarante	*karōnt*
50	cinquante	*sānkōnt*
60	soixante	*swassōnt*
70	soixante-dix	*swassōnt-deess*
80	quatre-vingts	*katr-vān*
90	quatre-vingt-dix	*katr-vān-deess*
91	quatre-vingt-onze	*katr-vān-ōnz*
100	cent	*sōn*
101	cent un	*sōn ān*
200	deux cents	*duh sōn*
202	deux cent deux	*duh sōn duh*

1,000	mille *meel*
2,000	deux mille *duh meel*
1,000,000	un million *ān meel-yōn*

1st	premier *pruhmyay*
2nd	deuxième *duhz-yem*
3rd	troisième *trwaz-yem*

87 plus 36.
Quatre-vingt-sept plus trente-six.
katr-vān-set plews trōnt-seess

800 minus 132
Huit cents moins cent trente-deux.
weet sōn mwān sōn trōnt-duh

22 times 15.
Vingt-deux fois quinze.
vān-duh fwa kānz

134 divided by 3.
Cent trente-quatre divisé par trois.
sōn trōnt-katr deeveezay par trwa

Fourteen and a half.
Quatorze et demie.
katorz ay duhmee

Twelve and a quarter.
Douze un quart.
dooz ān kar

Twelve and three quarters.
Douze trois quarts.
dooz trwa kar

35 point five, 3.5.
Trente-cinq virgule cinq, 3,5.
trōnt-sānk veergewl sānk

36 point seven five.
Trente-six virgule soixante-quinze.
trônt-seess veergewl swassônt-kânz

10%
Dix pour cent.
dee poor sôn

Half as much.
La moitié.
la mwatee-ay

Three times as much.
Trois fois plus.
trwa fwa plew

How many?
Combien ?
kômb-yân

How much?
Combien?
kômb-yân

More than 500.
Plus de cinq cents.
plew duh sânk sôn

Less than 50.
Moins de cinquante.
mwân duh sânkônt

OFFERING

Can I help?
Je peux aider ?
juh puh ayday

May I ...?
Je peux ... ?
juh puh

Let me.
Laissez-moi faire.
lessay-mwa fair

I'll do that for you.
Je vais vous le faire.
juh vay voo luh fair

It's no problem.
Il n'y a pas de problème.
eel n-ya pa duh prob-lem

My pleasure.
Le plaisir est pour moi.
luh plezzeer ay poor mwa

Would you like one?
Vous en voulez un ?
vo zōn voolay ān

Please take one.
Servez-vous.
sairvay-voo

Please, go on.
Allez-y, je vous en prie.
alay-zee juh voo zōn pree

Take mine.
Prenez le mien/la mienne.
pruhnay luh mee-ān/la mee-en

PAST TENSE

To put something into the past tense, to say that you HAVE DONE or DID DO something, you use the forms of the verb **avoir** plus the past participle of the verb:

avoir

j'ai	*jay*	I have
tu as	*tew a*	you have
il/elle a	*eel/el a*	he/she/it has
nous avons	*noo zavoñ*	we have
vous avez	*voo zavay*	you have
ils/elles ont	*eel/el zoñ*	they have

As a basic rule for forming the past participle: for verbs ending in **-er**, change **-er** to **-é** (pronunciation the same: *ay*); for verbs ending in **-ir**, change **-ir** to **-i**; for verbs ending in **-re**, change **-re** to **-u**.

Where did you buy that?
Où est-ce que vous avez acheté cela?
oo eskuh voo zavay ashuhtay suhla

I found it at the market.
Je l'ai trouvé au marché.
juh lay troovay o marshay

I've finished.
J'ai fini
jay feenee

We sold it.
Nous l'avons vendu.
noo lavoñ voñdew

For some common and important verbs the past tense is formed using **être** instead of **avoir**. These verbs are marked up in the dictionary section with an asterisk.

être

		(literal sense)
je suis	*juh swee*	I am
tu es	*tew ay*	you are
il/elle est	*eel/el ay*	he/she/it is
nous sommes	*noo som*	we are
vous êtes	*voo zet*	you are
ils/elles sont	*eel/el sōn*	they are

He has gone out.
Il est sorti.
eel ay·sortee

We arrived last week.
Nous sommes arrivés la semaine dernière.
noo som zareevay la suhmen dairn-yair

I went to Paris.
Je suis allé à Paris.
juh swee zalay a paree

They've left.
Ils sont partis.
eel sōn partee

Two common verbs in another past tense ('was' and 'had'):

I was	**j'étais**	*jaytay*
you were	**tu étais**	*tew aytay*
he/she/it was	**il/elle était**	*eel/el aytay*
we were	**nous étions**	*noo zaytee-ōn*
you were	**vous étiez**	*voo zaytee-ay*
they were	**ils/elles étaient**	*eel/el zaytay*

I had	**j'avais**	*javay*
you had	**tu avais**	*tew avay*
he/she/it had	**il/elle avait**	*eel/el avay*
we had	**nous avions**	*noo zavee-ōn*
you had	**vous aviez**	*voo zavee-ay*
they had	**ils/elles avaient**	*eel/el zavay*

91

PERMISSION

Can I ...?
Je peux ...?
juh puh

Can we ...?
Nous pouvons ...?
noo poovoñ

Can he/she ...?
Il/elle peut ...?
eel/el puh

Can they ...?
Ils/elles peuvent ... ?
eel/el purv

Can I go in?
Je peux entrer ?
juh puh oñtray

Is it allowed?
C'est permis ?
say pairmee

Is that all right?
Est-ce que ça va ?
eskuh sa va

That's ok, on you go.
Ça va, allez-y.
sa va alay-zee

Can you give me a permit?
Vous pouvez me donner une autorisation ?
voo poovay muh donnay ewn otoreezass-yoñ

PHOTOGRAPHS

Do you have a film for this camera?
Avez-vous une pellicule pour cet appareil photo ?
avay-voo ewn peleekewl poor set aparay foto

35mm/16mm.
trente-cinq millimètres/seize millimètres.
trõnt-sãnk meeleemetr/sez meeleemetr

12/24/36 exposures.
Douze/vingt-quatre/trente-six poses.
dooz/vãn-katr/trõnt-seess pohz

Can you develop these?
Pouvez-vous développer celles-là ?
poovay-voo dayvelopay sel-la

I'd like prints/slides.
Je voudrais des photos papier/des diapositives.
juh voodray day foto pap-yay/day dee-apozeeteev

Can you give me another print of these two?
Pouvez-vous me faire une autre épreuve de ces deux-là ?
poovay-voo muh fair ewn ohtr ayprurv duh say duh-la

Excuse me, could you take a photograph of me/us?
Excusez-moi, vous voulez bien me/nous prendre en photo ?
ex-kewzay-mwa voo voolay b-yãn muh/noo prõndr õn foto

Smile!
Souriez !
sooree-ay

Tirage en une heure
teerahj õn ewn ur
One-hour film processing service

PLURALS

The most common way of forming the plural of a noun, of saying THE RESTAURANTS instead of THE RESTAURANT, is by adding an **-s** to the singular:

The restaurant. Le restaurant. *luh restoroñ*	**The restaurants.** Les restaurants. *lay restoroñ*
The café. Le café. *luh kafay*	**The cafés.** Les cafés. *lay kafay*

Note that this **-s** is not normally pronounced in French.

To make the plural of words ending in **-au** or **-eu** you add an **-x**:

The boat. Le bateau. *luh bato*	**The boats.** Les bateaux. *lay bato*
A game. Un jeu. *añ juh*	**Four games.** Quatre jeux. *katr juh*

Note that this **-x** is not pronounced in French.

To make the plural of words ending in **-al** change **-al** to **-aux**:

A newspaper. Un journal. *añ joornal*	**Two newspapers.** Deux journaux. *duh joorno*

One important irregular plural:

My eye. Mon œil. *moñ ur-ee*	**My eyes.** Mes yeux. *may juh*

POLICE AND THE LAW

(see also CAR ACCIDENTS, THEFT)

Could you come with me, there's been some trouble.
Vous pouvez venir avec moi, il y a un problème.
voo poovay vuhneer avek mwa eel ya an prob-lem

He started it.
Il a commencé.
eel a komonsay

It wasn't my fault.
Je ne suis pas responsable.
juh nuh swee pa responsahbl

It was his/her fault.
Il/elle est responsable.
eel/el ay responsahbl

RESPONSES

Vos papiers.
vo pap-yay
Your documents.

Votre nom, s'il vous plaît ?
votr nom seel voo play
Your name please?

Votre adresse ?
votr adress
Your address?

Je peux voir votre passeport ?
juh puh vwahr votr passpor
Can I see your passport?

I didn't know it wasn't allowed.
Je ne savais pas que ce n'était pas permis.
juh nuh savay pa kuh suh naytay pa pairmee

There's no sign up.
Il n'y a pas de signe.
eel n-ya pa duh seen-yuh

It's not mine, I rented it.
Ça n'est pas le mien/la mienne, je l'ai loué(e).
sa nay pa luh mee-āñ/la mee-en juh lay looay

I want to report a loss.
Je voudrais faire une déclaration de perte.
juh voodray fair ewn dayklarass-yōñ duh pairt

... has gone missing.
... a disparu.
... a deesparew

He/she was wearing ...
Il/elle portait ...
eel/el portay

He/she has blue/brown eyes.
Il/elle a les yeux bleus/marron.
eel/el a lay juh bluh/marōñ

He/she has blonde hair.
Il/elle est blond/blonde.
eel/el ay blōñ/blōnd

He/she has red hair.
Il/elle est roux/rousse.
eel/el ay roo/rooss

96

POSSESSIVES

If you want to say that this is YOUR car or HIS car or HER car etc then you use the following words in French. Notice that there are three forms: one for masculine words (given with **le** in the dictionary); one for feminine words (given with **la** in the dictionary); and one for plural words.

	masculine	*feminine*	*plural*
my	**mon** *mōn*	**ma** *ma*	**mes** *may*
your	**ton** *tōn*	**ta** *ta*	**tes** *tay*
his/its	**son** *sōn*	**sa** *sa*	**ses** *say*
her/its	**son** *sōn*	**sa** *sa*	**ses** *say*
our	**notre** *notr*	**notre** *notr*	**nos** *no*
your	**votre** *votr*	**votre** *votr*	**vos** *vo*
their	**leur** *lur*	**leur** *lur*	**leurs** *lur*

Some points to note:

The forms **ton/ta/tes** are used for people you are speaking to as **tu**. The forms **votre/vos** are used for people you are speaking to as **vous** (*see* PRONOUNS).

Ma/ta/sa change to **mon/ton/son** in front of a vowel:

Mon amie.
mōn amee
My girlfriend.

Whether you use **son/sa** or **mon/ma** depends on the gender of the thing/person 'possessed'. So for example:

Ma voiture.
ma vwatewr
My car.

can be said by both a man and a woman. Likewise

Sa voiture.
sa vwatewr

can mean either 'his car' or 'her car'.

If this is confusing you can say:

Sa voiture à lui.
sa vwatewr a lwee
His car.

Sa voiture à elle.
sa vwatewr a el
Her car.

POSSIBILITIES

Is it possible to ...?
Est-il possible de ... ?
ayteel poseebl duh

Could I possibly borrow this?
Puis-je emprunter ceci ?
pwee-juh ōmprāntay suhsee

I might, I'm not sure.
Peut-être, je ne suis pas sûr(e).
puh-tetr juh nuh swee pa sewr

We might want to stay longer.
Nous voudrons peut-être rester plus longtemps.
noo voodrōn puh-tetr restay plew lōntōm

He might have.
Peut-être.
puh-tetr

They might have left already.
Ils sont peut-être déjà partis.
eel sōn puh-tetr day-ja partee

Who knows?
Qui sait ?
kee say

There's an outside chance.
Il y a une dernière chance.
eel ya ewn dairn-yair shōnss

That's out of the question!
C'est hors de question !
say tor duh kest-yōn

POST OFFICE

Two stamps for letters to the UK please.
Deux timbres pour lettre pour la Grande-Bretagne,
  s'il vous plaît.
duh tãmbr poor letr poor la grõn-bruhtan-yuh seel voo play

Eight stamps for postcards to England please.
Huit timbres pour carte postale pour l'Angleterre, s'il
  vous plaît.
weet tãmbr poor kart postahl poor lõngltair seel voo play

Do you have three aerogrammes?
Auriez-vous trois aérogrammes ?
oree-ay-voo trwa a-airogram

I'd like to send this registered.
Je voudrais envoyer cela en recommandé.
juh voodray õnvwi-yay suhla õn ruhkomõnday

Is there any mail for me?
Est-ce qu'il y a du courrier pour moi ?
eskeel ya dew kooree-ay poor mwa

YOU'LL SEE

Autres destinations.
ohtr destinass-yõn
All other places.

Etranger.
aytrõnjay
Overseas.

PTT (Postes, Télégraphes, Téléphones).
pay-tay-tay
French post office (and telephone company).

Timbres.
tãmbr
Stamps.

Prochaine levée.
proshen luhvay
Next collection.

PRACTISING YOUR FRENCH

Here are twenty questions about French. All of them can be answered by using the information given in the various sections of this book. The answers are on the next page.

1. What is the French for 'we are'?
2. What is the plural of **la voiture/le feu**?
3. What is the French for 'we can'?
4. **Je suis fatigué** means 'I am tired'. What is 'I am not tired'?
5. What is the feminine of the adjectives **froid/chaud/heureux**?
6. How do you say 'of the restaurant/of the cars'?
7. **Vous** is the polite pronoun for 'you'. What is the familiar pronoun?
8. **Facile** means 'easy'. How do you say 'easier'?
9. How do you say 'bigger than that'?
10. What is the French for 'on Tuesdays'?
11. What do the signs stationnement interdit/tirer mean?
12. If you order a **grand crème** to drink what will you get?
13. How would you ask for a single room for two nights?
14. How do you ask for the bill in a restaurant?
15. What is **poule**?
16. **Je suis très content** means 'I'm very pleased'. Say 'I was very pleased'.
17. How do you say 'I come from . . .'?
18. How do you ask someone their name?
19. If someone says 'thanks very much' to you in French what could you reply?
20. How do you pronounce **puis/quoi/faux/Marseille**?

PRACTISING YOUR FRENCH – ANSWERS

1. Nous sommes.
2. Les voitures, les feux.
3. Nous pouvons.
4. Je ne suis pas fatigué.
5. Froide/chaude/heureuse.
6. Du restaurant/des voitures.
7. Tu.
8. Plus facile.
9. Plus grand que ça.
10. Le mardi.
11. No parking/pull.
12. A large white coffee.
13. Vous avez une chambre pour une personne pour deux nuits ?
14. L'addition, s'il vous plaît.
15. Chicken.
16. J'étais très content.
17. Je viens de . . .
18. Comment vous appelez-vous ?
19. Je vous en prie.
20. *pwee/kwa/fo/marsay*

PRESENT TENSE

To form the present tense of a verb, to say that you
ARE DOING something or that something
HAPPENS etc you need to know the following verb
forms. The main types of verb end in **-er**, **-ir** and **-re**.

donner (to give)

je donne	*juh don*	I give
tu donnes	*tew don*	you give
il/elle donne	*eel/el don*	he/she/it gives
nous donnons	*noo donnōn*	we give
vous donnez	*voo donnay*	you give
ils/elles donnent	*eel/el don*	they give

finir (to finish)

je finis	*juh feenee*	I finish
tu finis	*tew feenee*	you finish
il/elle finit	*eel/el feenee*	he/she/it finishes
nous finissons	*noo feeneesōn*	we finish
vous finissez	*voo feeneesay*	you finish
ils/elles finissent	*eel/el feeneess*	they finish

attendre (to wait)

j'attends	*jatōn*	I wait
tu attends	*tew atōn*	you wait
il/elle attend	*eel/el atōn*	he/she/it waits
nous attendons	*noo zatōndōn*	we wait
vous attendez	*voo zatōnday*	you wait
ils/elles attendent	*eel/el zatōn*	they wait

Note that this tense also covers English expressions
like I AM WAITING etc.

We're waiting for you.
Nous vous attendons.
noo voo zatōndōn

Here are some useful verbs which end in **-ir** but which do not follow the general pattern as shown above:

partir (to leave)

je pars	*juh par*	I leave
tu pars	*tew par*	you leave
il/elle part	*eel/el par*	he/she/it leaves
nous partons	*noo partōn*	we leave
vous partez	*voo partay*	you leave
ils/elles partent	*eel/el part*	they leave

sortir (to go out)

je sors	*juh sor*	I go out
tu sors	*tew sor*	you go out
il/elle sort	*eel/el sor*	he/she/it goes out
nous sortons	*noo sortōn*	we go out
vous sortez	*voo sortay*	you go out
ils/elles sortent	*eel/el sort*	they go out

dormir (to sleep)

je dors	*juh dor*	I sleep
tu dors	*tew dor*	you sleep
il/elle dort	*eel/el dor*	he/she/it sleeps
nous dormons	*noo dormōn*	we sleep
vous dormez	*voo dormay*	you sleep
ils/elles dorment	*eel/el dorm*	they sleep

Tenir behaves in the same way as **venir**.

Some common verbs have irregular forms in the present tense (See also PAST TENSE for **avoir** and **être**):

aller (to go)

je vais	*juh vay*	I go
tu vas	*tew va*	you go
il/elle va	*eel/el va*	he/she/it goes
nous allons	*noo zalōn*	we go
vous allez	*voo zalay*	you go
ils/elles vont	*eel/el vōn*	they go

venir (to come)

je viens	*juh v-yān*	I come
tu viens	*tew v-yān*	you come
il/elle vient	*eel/el v-yān*	he/she/it comes
nous venons	*noo vuhnōn*	we come
vous venez	*voo vuhnay*	you come
ils/elles viennent	*eel/el v-yen*	they come

vouloir (to want)

je veux	*juh vuh*	I want
tu veux	*tew vuh*	you want
il/elle veut	*eel/el vuh*	he/she/it wants
nous voulons	*noo voolōn*	we want
vous voulez	*voo voolay*	you want
lis/elles veulent	*eel/el vurl*	they want

pouvoir (to be able to)

je peux	*juh puh*	I can
tu peux	*tew puh*	you can
il/elle peut	*eel/el puh*	he/she/it can
nous pouvons	*noo poovōn*	we can
vous pouvez	*voo poovay*	you can
ils/elles peuvent	*eel/el purv*	they can

PRONOUNS

If you are using a pronoun as the subject of a verb, saying 'HE is' or 'WE are' or 'can YOU?' etc, the words are:

je	*juh*	I	**nous**	*noo*	we
tu	*tew*	you	**vous**	*voo*	you
il	*eel*	he/it	**ils**	*eel*	they
elle	*el*	she/it	**elles**	*el*	they

Points to note:

YOU: **tu** is used when speaking to someone who is a friend, or to someone of your own general age group with whom you want to establish a friendly atmosphere. **Vous** is used when speaking to several friends (ie it is the plural of **tu**) or it is used when speaking to someone you don't know. In the vast majority of cases when travelling as a foreigner in France you will use the **vous** form. Certainly, if you are in any doubt as to which form to use, choose the **vous** form.

IT: if you are using 'it' to refer to something like 'the car', 'the train' etc (as opposed to saying 'it is cold today' etc) you should use either **il** or **elle** depending on the gender of the thing you are talking about. (*See ARTICLES*). For example, **la voiture** (the car) is **elle** (it) and **le train** (the train) is **il** (it).

If you are using the pronoun as an object, saying 'I know HIM' or 'he saw THEM' etc, use the following words:

me	*muh*	me	**nous**	*noo*	us
te	*tuh*	you	**vous**	*voo*	you
le	*luh*	him/it	**les**	*lay*	them
la	*la*	her/it			

I know him.		**He saw them.**
Je le connais.		Il les a vus.
juh luh konay		*eel lay za vew*

Can you hear me?
Vous m'entendez ?
voo mōntōnday

If you are using a pronoun to say, for example, you sent something TO HER or that you spoke TO HIM, then use the following words:

me	*muh*	to me	**nous**	*noo*	to us
te	*tuh*	to you	**vous**	*voo*	to you
lui	*lwee*	to him/her/it	**leur**	*lur*	to them

I spoke to him.		**I gave it to him.**
Je lui ai parlé.		Je le lui ai donné.
juh lwee ay parlay		*juh luh lwee ay donnay*

If you are using a pronoun to say 'it's ME, 'with HER', 'for THEM' etc, then use these words:

moi	*mwa*	me	**nous**	*noo*	us
toi	*twa*	you	**vous**	*voo*	you
lui	*lwee*	him	**eux**	*uh*	them
elle	*el*	her	**elles**	*el*	them

Who's that? – It's me.		**This is for you.**
Qui c'est? – C'est moi.		C'est pour toi/vous.
kee say – say mwa		*say poor twa/voo*

After him/us.
Après lui/nous.
apray lwee/noo

A useful word for 'it' is **ça** *sa*.

PRONUNCIATION

The following general guidelines to special sounds will
help you pronounce new French words that you
encounter. To get the actual values of the sounds listen
carefully to a French speaker and try to copy what you
hear. (*See also the INTRODUCTION*).

é	as in day (Elysée, allé)
è/ê	as in fed (Genève, Liège, même)
u/û	prepare your mouth for oo, but then say ee (du, salut)
ai/eil/er/et/ez	as in day (j'ai, sommeil, Montpellier, cabinet, allez)
ail	as in eye (travail)
ain/aim/ein/ in/im/un/um	as ang in sang but without pronouncing the ng (main, faim, plein, vin, timbre, un)
an/am/en/em/ on/om	as ong in song but without pronouncing the ng (maman, chambre, Rouen, novembre, mon, sombre)
au/eau	as in go (chaud, peau)
eu/œu	as the e in mother (peu, noeud)
ien	as in Yan but without pronouncing the n
oi/ois	as in 'wa' (moi, mois, quoi)
oin	as in Wang but without pronouncing the g (loin, soin)
ou/où/oû	as in moon (fou, où, coûter)
ou	if before a vowel then pronounced w (oui)
ui	pronounced as we (suis, puis)

In addition to the combinations shown above, a number of letters are silent in French. If the following come at the end of a word then you do not pronounce them as separate sounds: d, s, t, x.

Paris *paree*　　　　**met** *may*　　　　**faux** *foh*

But if there is an e after these letters then they are sounded:

chaud *shoh*　　　　　　**chaude** *shohd*
tout *too*　　　　　　　**toute** *toot*

Finally remember that French r's come from the back of the throat.

QUESTIONS

What is ...?
Qu'est-ce que c'est ... ?
keskuh say

What's this?
Qu'est-ce que c'est ?
keskuh say

Where is ...?
Où est ... ?
oo ay

When is ...?
C'est quand ... ?
say kōn

Which is ...?
Lequel/laquelle est ... ?
luhkel/lakel ay

Who is ...?
Qui est ... ?
kee ay

Why ...?
Pourquoi ... ?
poorkwa

How long will it take?
Ça prendra combien de temps ?
sa prōndra kōmb-yān duh tōm

How do I get to ...?
Comment aller à ... ?
komōn alay a

How do you do it?
Comment on fait ?
komon on fay

What are these?
Qu'est-ce que c'est ?
keskuh say

Where are we going?
Où va-t-on ?
oo vaton

Which are mine?
Lesquel(le)s sont à moi ?
laykel son ta mwa

Can you tell me …?
Vous pouvez me dire … ?
voo poovay muh deer

Can you …?
Pouvez-vous … ?
poovay-voo

Can I …?
Je peux … ?
juh puh

Can we …?
Nous pouvons … ?
noo poovon

Can he/she …?
Il/elle peut … ?
eel/el puh

Could you write it down?
Vous pouvez l'écrire ?
voo poovay laykreer

REFERRING TO THINGS/PEOPLE

This one.
Celui-ci/celle-ci.
suh-lwee-see/sel-see

That one.
Celui-là/celle-là.
suh-lwee-la/sel-la

Not that one, the one behind it.
Non pas celui-là, celui qui est derrière.
nōn pa suh-lwee-la suhlwee kee ay dair-yair

That one over there.
Celui-là, là-bas.
suh-lwee-la la-ba

The man over there.
Cet homme, là-bas
set om la-ba

Him/her.
Lui/elle.
lwee/el

Him in the green shirt.
Lui, avec la chemise verte.
lwee avek la shuhmeez vairt

The woman next to her.
La femme à côté d'elle.
la fam a kohtay del

These two/those two.
Ces deux-là.
say duh la

No no, the other one.
Non, non, l'autre.
nōn nōn lohtr

112

RENTALS

I want to hire a car/bike/moped.
Je voudrais louer une voiture/une moto/une mobylette.
juh voodray loo-ay ewn vwatewr/ewn moto/ewn mobeelet

Can I rent one for a day/two days/a week?
Je peux la louer pour une journée/deux jours/une
  semaine ?
juh puh la loo-ay poor ewn joornay/duh joor/ewn suhmen

How much is it per day?
C'est combien par jour ?
say kōmb-yān par joor

When do we have to bring it back?
Il faut la ramener quand ?
eel fo la ramnay kōn

RESPONSES

Votre carte d'identité.
votr kart deedōnteetay
Your identity card. (passport will do)

Votre permis de conduire.
votr pairmee duh kōndweer
Your driving licence.

Votre adresse en France ?
votr adress ōn frōnss
Your address in France?

I'm at Hotel ...
Je suis à l'hôtel ...
juh swee a lotel

It's rented.
C'est loué.
say loo-ay

REPAIRS

Can you fix this?
Vous pouvez réparer ça ?
voo poovay rayparay sa

It's broken.
C'est cassé.
say kassay

Can you put new soles on these?
Vous pouvez les ressemeler ?
voo poovay lay ruhsuhmuhlay

Can you re-heel these?
Vous pouvez refaire le talon ?
voo poovay ruhfair luh talōn

Can you put a patch on this?
Vous pouvez mettre une pièce là-dessus ?
voo poovay metr ewn p-yess la-duhsew

Can you replace this?
Vous pouvez remplacer ça ?
voo poovay rōmplassay sa

It needs a new ...
Il faudrait un/une autre ...
eel fohdray ān/ewn ohtr

Can you do it today/by tomorrow?
Vous pouvez le faire aujourd'hui/pour demain ?
voo poovay luh fair o-joordwee/poor duhmān

Can you write the price down please?
Vous pouvez écrire le prix, s'il vous plaît ?
voo poovay aykreer luh pree seel voo play

114

REQUESTS

Could you please ...?
Pourriez-vous, s'il vous plaît ... ?
pooree-ay-voo seel voo play

Could you tell me ...?
Pourriez-vous me dire ...?
pooree-ay-voo muh deer

Could you give this to her?
Pourriez-vous lui donner cela ?
pooree-ay-voo lwee donnay suhla

Could I ...?
Est-ce que je peux ...?
eskuh juh puh

Could I have ...?
Est-ce que je peux avoir ...?
eskuh juh puh avwahr

Could we have another?
Est-ce que nous pouvons en avoir un/une autre ?
eskuh noo poovon zon avwahr an/ewn ohtr

Please leave it open.
Laissez le/la ouvert(e).
lessay luh/la oovair(t)

Please don't.
Non, je vous en prie.
non juh voo zon pree

Please don't speak so fast.
S'il vous plaît, ne parlez pas si vite.
seel voo play nuh parlay pa see veet

RESTAURANTS

(see MENU READER and DICTIONARY)

A table for one/for three please.
Une table pour une personne/pour trois, s'il vous plaît.
ewn tahbl poor ewn pairson/poor trwa seel voo play

Can we have a table outside/inside?
Nous pouvons avoir une table dehors/dedans ?
noo poovōn avvwahr ewn tahbl duh-or/duh-dōn

Can I book a table for this evening?
Je peux réserver une table pour ce soir ?
juh puh rayzairvay ewn tahbl poor suh swahr

I've booked a table.
J'ai réservé une table.
jay rayzairvay ewn tahbl

The name is ...
C'est au nom de ...
say to nōm duh

Can I see the menu?
Je peux voir le menu ?
juh puh vwahr luh muhnew

Can I see the wine list please?
Je peux voir la liste des vins, s'il vous plaît ?
juh puh vwahr la leest day vān seel voo play

Can we have the set menu for two?
Nous pouvons avoir le menu du jour pour deux ?
noo poovōn avvwahr luh muhnew dew joor poor duh

A bottle of house red please.
Une bouteille de vin rouge de la maison, s'il vous plaît.
ewn bootay duh vān rooj duh la mezzōn seel voo play

Waiter!/Miss!
Garçon !/Mademoiselle !
garsōn/mad-mwazel

That's for me thanks.
C'est pour moi merci.
say poor mwa mairsee.

That's for him/her.
C'est pour lui/elle.
say poor lweelel

I didn't order this.
Je n'ai pas commandé cela.
juh nay pa komōnday suhla

I ordered red wine.
J'ai commandé du vin rouge.
jay komōnday dew vān rooj

I'm afraid this tastes funny.
Il me semble que cela a un drôle de goût.
eel muh sōmbl kuh suhla a ān drohl duh goo

Can we see the dessert trolley?
Nous pouvons voir le chariot des desserts ?
noo poovōn vwahr luh sharee-o day dezzair

Two coffees please.
Deux cafés, s'il vous plaît.
duh kafay seel voo play

One cappuccino and one espresso.
Un café crème et un café noir.
ān kafay krem ay ān kafay nwahr

A cup of tea please.
Un thé au lait, s'il vous plaît.
ān tay o lay seel voo play

That was absolutely excellent!
C'était vraiment délicieux !
saytay vraymōn dayleess-yuh

Can I have the bill please?
L'addition, s'il vous plaît.
ladeess-yōn seel voo play

ROAD SIGNS

aire de repos rest area
allumez vos phares switch your headlights on
arrêtez votre moteur switch your engine off
attention fourrière illegally parked vehicles will be towed
 away
attention piétons beware of pedestrians
attention travaux caution: roadworks
attention verglas beware of ice
brouillard fréquent danger of fog
cassis ramp
chaussée déformée uneven road surface
chaussée inondée road flooded
chaussée rétrécie road narrows
chemin privé private road
chute de pierres falling rocks
circulez sur une file single line traffic
contrôle radar radar speed checks
convoi exceptionnel long vehicle
défense de ... no ...
dénivellation ramp
déviation detour
dos d'âne bumps in road surface
éteignez vos phares switch off your headlights
horodateur parking meter
interdiction d'entrer no entry
interdiction de stationner no parking
itinéraire bis alternative route
jours pairs/impairs park this side on even/odd days of the
 month
parking non gardé unsupervised parking
parking payant pay to park here
péage toll
ralentissez slow down
route barrée road blocked
sauf riverains access only
sortie de véhicules/camions vehicle/lorry exit
stationnement gênant no parking
stationnement interdit parking forbidden
ticket/disque obligatoire pay and display
toutes directions all directions
virage dangereux dangerous bend
voie sans issue no through road

ROOMS – FINDING A ROOM

(see also HOTELS)

I'm looking for a room.
Je cherche une chambre.
juh shairsh ewn shombr

Where I can find a room that's not too expensive?
Où puis-je trouver une chambre qui ne soit pas trop chère?
oo pwee-juh troovay ewn shombr kee nuh swa pa tro shair

What's a good area for finding a room?
Quel est le meilleur quartier pour trouver une chambre ?
kel ay luh may-ur kart-yay poor troovay ewn shombr

Just one night.
Une nuit seulement.
ewn nwee surlmon

Just one person/there are two of us.
Une personne seulement/nous sommes deux.
ewn pairson surlmon/noo som duh

Could you write the address down for me?
Pouvez-vous écrire l'adresse, s'il vous plaît ?
poovay-voo aykreer ladress seel voo play

Could you ring them from here to check?
Vous pourriez leur téléphoner pour vérifier ?
voo pooree-ay lur taylayfonay poor vayreefee-ay

RESPONSES

Tout est complet en ville.	**Essayez …**
too tay komplay on veel	*essay-ay*
The town is absolutely full up.	Try …

SELF-CATERING APARTMENTS

Could you check the cooker/fridge/shower?
Vous voulez bien vérifier la cuisinière/le frigidaire/la douche ?
voo voolay b-yان vayreefee-ay la kweeseen-yair/luh freejeedair/la doosh

How does the ... work?
Comment ça marche, le/la ...
komon sa marsh luh/la

The maid wasn't there today.
La femme de chambre n'est pas venue aujourd'hui.
la fam duh shombr nay pa vuhnew o-joordwee

The people next door to us make a terrible noise.
Les gens d'à côté font un bruit insupportable.
lay jon dakohtay fon ān brwee ānsewportahbl

Could you maybe have a quiet word with them?
Vous pourriez peut-être leur en parler gentiment ?
voo pooree-ay puhtetr lur on parlay jonteemon

When does the shop open/close?
A quelle heure ouvre/ferme le magasin ?
a kel ur oovr/fairm luh magazان

Could we have some clean bedding?
Nous pourrions avoir des draps propres ?
noo pooree-on avwahr day dra propr

Thank you for looking after us.
Merci de votre gentillesse.
mairsee duh votr jontee-ess

SHOPPING

I've got some shopping to do.
J'ai des courses à faire.
jay day koorss a fair

He's gone to the shops.
Il est allé faire des courses.
eel ay talay fair day koorss

Do you have ...?
Vous avez ... ?
voo zavay

I'm just looking thanks.
Je ne fais que regarder, merci.
juh nuh fay kuh ruhgarday mairsee

Can I have a look around?
Je peux regarder ?
juh puh ruhgarday

How much is this?
C'est combien ?
say komb-yān

Do you have other colours?
Vous l'avez en d'autres couleurs ?
voo lavay ōn dohtr koolur

Do you have any smaller ones?
Vous en avez de plus petits ?
voo zōn avay duh plew puhtee

Do you have any bigger ones?
Vous en avez de plus grands ?
voo zōn avay duh plew grōn

It's not really what I'm looking for.
Ce n'est pas vraiment ce que je veux.
suh nay pa vraymōn suh kuh juh vuh

121

That's fine, I'll take it.
C'est très bien, je le prends.
say tray b-yañ juh luh prôñ

Could you gift-wrap it for me?
Vous pouvez me faire un emballage-cadeau, s'il vous
plaît ?
voo poovay muh fair añ ōmbalahj-kado seel voo play

Can I use this? (credit card)
Je peux payer avec ça ?
juh puh pay-ay avek sa

SIGNS

Soldes
solld
Sale

Liquidation
leekeedass-yōñ
Clearance sale

Prix réduits
pree raydwee
Bargain prices

SHOP NAMES

Boucherie *booshuree* Butcher's
Boulangerie *boolōñjuhree* Baker's
Bureau de tabac *bewro duh taba* Newsagent's and
tobacconist's (also sells stamps and phonecards)
Cordonnier *kordon-yay* Shoe repairs
Epicerie *aypeesuhree* Grocer's
Librairie-papeterie *leebrairee-papuhtree* Bookshop and
stationer's
Pressing *presseeng* Dry cleaner's

SIGHTSEEING

Do you have a map of the area?
Avez-vous une carte de la région ?
avay-voo ewn kart duh la ray-jōn

Do you have a guidebook for the area?
Avez-vous un guide touristique de la région ?
avay-voo an geed tooreesteek duh la ray-jōn

Are there any guided tours (of the city/the area)?
Il y a des visites guidées (de la ville/de la région) ?
eel ya day veezeet geeday (duh la veel/duh la ray-jōn)

We want to go to ...
Nous voulons aller à ...
noo voolōn zalay a

We've been seeing the sights.
Nous avons visité les endroits touristiques.
noo zavōn veezeetay lay zōndrwa tooreesteek

I want to see the real Paris/France.
Je veux voir le vrai Paris/la vraie France.
juh vuh vwahr luh vray paree/la vray frōnss

Can you give us the name of a really typical restaurant?
Pouvez-vous nous indiquer le nom d'un restaurant typique ?
poovay-voo noo zāndeekay luh nōm dān restorōn teepeek

Syndicat d'initiative.
Tourist information office.

Visite guidée de la ville.
Guided city tour.

Bateaux mouches.
Sightseeing boats on the Seine.

SIGNS

à louer to rent
à vendre for sale
accès aux quais to the platforms
accès interdit no entry
accueil reception
achat buying rate
affranchissements stamps
alimentation food, grocer's
appellation contrôlée mark guaranteeing the quality of a wine
arrondissement an administrative district of Paris
attachez vos ceintures fasten your seat belt
attention chien méchant beware of the dog
attention fermeture automatique des portières caution: doors close automatically
baignade dangereuse danger: do not swim here
baignade interdite no swimming
bienvenue à ... welcome to ...
brasserie pub, bar
caisse d'épargne savings bank
carte orange season ticket
cédez le passage give way
chèque de voyage traveller's cheque
compostez votre billet stamp your ticket in the machine
consigne left luggage
correspondance connection
cours de change exchange rate
dames ladies
défense d'afficher stick no bills
défense de déposer des ordures no litter, no tipping
défense de fumer no smoking
défense de marcher sur la pelouse keep off the grass
défense de parler au conducteur do not talk to the driver
dégustation de vin wine tasting
département administrative district of France
douane customs
droite right
eau non potable not drinking water
embarquement immédiat boarding now
en cas d'incendie in the event of fire
en cas d'urgence in an emergency
en dérangement out of order

enregistrement des bagages check-in
entrez sans frapper enter without knocking
faites l'appoint have the right change ready
fermé closed
fermeture annuelle annual holiday
frappez avant d'entrer knock before entering
fumeurs smokers
gare SNCF French railway station
gauche left
gîte rural rural holiday accommodation
grandes lignes main lines
gratuit free
heures de levée collection
horaire timetable
horaires d'ouverture opening times
hôtel de ville city hall
indicatif dialling code
interdit aux mineurs no admittance to those under 18 years
of age
itinéraire conseillé recommended route
journaux newspapers
jours ouvrables weekdays
la maison n'accepte pas les chèques we do not accept
cheques
lavomatic launderette
le compostage des billets est obligatoire tickets are valid
only if stamped
les articles soldés ne sont ni repris ni échangés no
refund or exchange of reduced price goods
location de voitures car hire
M metro
mairie town hall
Manche English Channel
messieurs gents
mode d'emploi directions for use
navette shuttle service
ne pas déranger do not disturb
non fumeurs non smoking
ouvert open
papiers litter
passage piétons pedestrian crossing
passage souterrain subway, underpass

payez à la caisse pay at the desk
pêche interdite no fishing
peinture fraîche wet paint
piscine swimming pool
place square
plage beach
poids lourds heavy vehicles
point de rencontre meeting point
police secours emergency services
pont bridge
pousser push
préfecture regional headquarters
prière de (ne pas) ... please (do not) ...
privé private
prochaine séance à ... heures next showing at ...
provenance from
relais routier transport café (often serving good quality food)
renseignements information
RE fast limited stop train in Paris
rien à déclarer nothing to declare
SA (société anonyme) Ltd
salle de bain bathroom
sans plomb lead-free
sortie exit
sous-titré with subtitles
SVP (s'il vous plaît) please
syndicat d'initiative tourist information centre
taille size
tarif des consommations price list
temple protestant church
TGV (train à grande vitesse) high speed train
tirer pull
tout compris all-inclusive
TTC (toutes taxes comprises) all taxes included
TVA (taxe sur la valeur ajoutée) VAT
valable jusqu'au ... valid until ...
vente selling rate
version originale, VO in the original language
voie platform
wagon lit sleeper

SMOKING

Can I have a packet of ...?
Je voudrais un paquet de ... ?
juh voodray an pakay duh

Have you got a light?
Vous avez du feu ?
voo zavay dew fuh

Do you mind if I smoke?
Ça vous dérange si je fume ?
sa voo dayronj see juh fewm

Do you smoke?
Vous fumez ?
voo fewmay

I've given up.
J'ai arrêté (de fumer).
jay aruhtay (duh fewmay)

Try one of these.
Vous connaissez ? prenez-en une.
voo konessay prenna-zon ewn

Excuse me, it's no smoking here.
Excusez-moi, c'est non-fumeurs ici.
ex-kewzay-mwa say nonfewmur ee-see

I quite enjoy the occasional cigar.
J'aime bien fumer un cigare à l'occasion.
jem b-yan fewmay an seegar a lokass-yon

Do you have any pipe tobacco?
Vous avez du tabac pour pipe ?
voo zavay dew taba poor peep

SPORT

Let's go to the swimming baths.
Allons à la piscine.
alon a la peeseen

Isn't there an outdoor pool?
Est-ce qu'il n'y a pas une piscine découverte ?
eskeel n-ya pa zewn peeseen daykoovairt

Is there a sports centre here?
Est-ce qu'il y a un centre sportif ici ?
eskeel ya an sontr sporteef ee-see

I'm going jogging – coming too?
Je vais faire un jogging – tu viens ?
juh vay fair an joggeeng tew v-yan

How about a game of tennis?
Et si on jouait au tennis ?
ay see on joo-ay o teness

Your serve.
A toi de servir.
a twa duh sairveer

Good shot!
Belle balle !
bel bal

I'd like to hire a sailboard.
Je voudrais louer une planche à voile.
juh voodray loo-ay ewn plonsh a vwal

Can we go sailing?
On peut faire de la voile ?
on puh fair duh la vwal

There's a football match on television.
Il y a un match de football à la télévision.
eel ya an match duh footbal a la taylayveez-yon

SUGGESTIONS

What do you suggest?
Qu'est-ce que vous proposez ?
keskuh voo propohzay

Let's go to the beach/cinema.
Allons à la plage/au cinéma.
alōn za la plahj/o seenayma

Let's leave.
Partons.
partōn

How about an ice cream/a beer?
Une glace/une bière, ça vous dit ?
ewn glass/ewn b-yair sa voo dee

Why don't we hire a car?
Et si on louait une voiture ?
ay see ōn loo-ay ewn vwatewr

Why don't you talk to her?
Et si vous lui parliez ?
ay see voo lwee parlee-ay

Why don't you complain about it?
Pourquoi vous n'allez pas vous plaindre ?
poorkwa voo nalay pa voo plāndr

You should tell the manager about it.
Vous devriez le dire au patron.
voo duhvree-ay luh deer o patrōn

How about it, what do you say?
Et ça, qu'est-ce que vous en dites ?
ay sa keskuh voo zōn deet

SURPRISE

What a surprise!
Quelle surprise !
kel sewrpreez

Well, look who it is!
Hé, regardez qui c'est !
hay ruhgarday kee say

Well well well!
Tiens tiens !
t-yan t-yan

Good heavens!
Mon dieu !
mon d-yuh

Struth!
Ça alors !
sa alor

That's amazing!
C'est incroyable !
say tankwri-yahbl

That's terrible!
C'est affreux !
say tafruh

I don't believe it!
C'est pas vrai !
say pa vray

How strange!
Comme c'est bizarre !
kom say beezar

TALKING ABOUT ONESELF

My name is ...
Je m'appelle ...
juh mapel

I am ... years old.
J'ai ... ans.
jay ... oñ

I'm a teacher/doctor/taxi-driver.
Je suis professeur/médecin/conducteur de taxi.
juh swee professur/maydsañ/koñdewktur duh taxee

I'm a hairdresser/nurse/head teacher. (female)
Je suis coiffeuse/infirmière/directrice d'école
juh swee kwafurz/añfairm-yair/deerektreess daykol

I come from ...
Je viens de ...
juh v-yañ duh

I was born in London/Ireland.
Je suis né(e) à Londres/en Irlande.
juh swee nay a loñdr/oñ eerloñd

I was born in 1956.
Je suis né(e) en 1956.
juh swee nay oñ meel-nuhf-soñ sañkoñ-seess

I'm single/I'm married.
Je suis célibataire/je suis marié(e).
juh swee sayleebatair/juh swee maree-ay

I'm separated/I'm divorced.
Je suis séparé(e)/je suis divorcé(e).
juh swee sayparay/juh swee deevorsay

I have two children.
J'ai deux enfants.
jay duh zoñfoñ

TALKING TO PEOPLE

What's your name?
Comment vous appelez-vous ?
kōmōn voo zaplay-voo

How old are you?
Vous avez quel âge ?
voo zavay kel ahj

What do you do?
Qu'est-ce que vous faites dans la vie ?
keskuh voo fet dōn la vee

Where do you come from?
D'où venez-vous ?
doo vuhnay-voo

Where do you live?
Où habitez-vous ?
oo abeetay-voo

Are you married?
Vous êtes marié(e) ?
voo zet maree-ay

Do you have any family?
Vous avez de la famille ?
voo zavay duh la famee

Have you ever been to Britain?
Vous êtes déjà allé(e) en Grande-Bretagne ?
voo zet dayja alay ōn grōnd-bruhtan-yuh

Do you speak English?
Vous parlez anglais ?
voo parlay ōnglay

TAXIS

Could you get me a taxi?
Vous pouvez m'appeler un taxi ?
voo poovay maplay an taxee

I'd like to book a taxi for tomorrow morning.
Je voudrais réserver un taxi pour demain matin.
juh voodray rayzairvay an taxee poor duhman matan

To the station/to the airport/to the Louvre.
A la gare/à l'aéroport/au Louvre.
a la gar/a lairopor/o loovr

How much is it going to cost?
Ça va coûter combien ?
sa va kootay komb-yan

Could you stop here?
Vous pouvez vous arrêter ici?
voo poovay voo zaretay ee-see

This is fine.
C'est parfait.
say parfay

Can you wait for me/us please?
Vous pouvez m'attendre/nous attendre, s'il vous plaît ?
voo poovay matondr/noo zatondr seel voo play

Can you take me/us back again?
Vous pouvez me/nous ramener ?
voo poovay muh/noo ramnay

Can you come back at ...?
Vous pouvez revenir à ... ?
voo poovay ruhvuhneer a

TELEPHONING

Can I use your phone?
Je peux me servir de votre téléphone ?
juh puh muh sairveer duh votr taylayfon

Hello, can I speak to …?
Allô, puis-je parler à …?
alo pwee-juh parlay a

RESPONSES

Une seconde, s'il vous plaît.
ewn suhgond seel voo play
Just a minute please.

C'est de la part de qui ?
say duh la par duh kee
Who shall I say is calling?

Qui est à l'appareil ?
kee ay ta laparay
Who's speaking?

Il/elle n'est pas là.
eel/el nay pa la
He/she's not here.

Ne quittez pas.
nuh keetay pa
Hold the line.

Can I leave a message?
Je peux laisser un message ?
juh puh lessay an messahj

Please tell him that … called.
Vous pouvez lui dire que … a appelé, s'il vous plaît.
voo poovay lwee deer kuh … a aplay seel voo play

I'm at Hotel . . . .
Je suis à l'hôtel . . .
juh swee a lohtel

My phone number is . . .
Mon numéro de téléphone est le . . .
mōn newmayro duh taylayfon ay luh

45 38 50 81.
le quarante cinq, trente huit, cinquante, quatre-vingt-un.
luh karōnt sānk trōnt weet sānkōnt katr vān ān

Can you ask him/her to call me back?
Vous pouvez lui demander de me rappeler?
voo poovay lwee duhmōnday duh muh raplay

YOU'LL SEE

Décrochez.
daykroshay
Lift the receiver.

Fermez le volet svp.
fairmay luh volay seel voo play
Please close the flap.

Introduire votre carte ou faire no. d'urgence
āntrodweer votr kart oo fair newmayro dewrjōnss
Insert your card or dial emergency number.

Numérotez.
newmayrotay
Dial.

Patientez.
pass-yōntay
Please wait.

THANKS

Thank you.
Merci.
mairsee

> **De rien, je vous en prie.**
> *duh r-yan̄ juh voo zōn pree*
> You're welcome.

Thanks a lot, thank you very much.
Merci beaucoup.
mairsee bohkoo

That's very kind of you.
C'est très gentil de votre part.
say tray jōntee duh votr par

No thanks, no thank you.
Non merci.
nōn mairsee

Not for me thanks.
Pas pour moi merci.
pa poor mwa mairsee

Thank you for everything.
Merci pour tout.
mairsee poor too

Many thanks for your help.
Merci beaucoup pour votre aide.
mairsee bohkoo poor votr ed

Could you thank him/her for me?
Vous pourrez le/la remercier de ma part ?
voo pooray luh/la ruhmairsee-ay duh ma par

He/she sends his/her thanks.
Il/elle vous remercie.
eel/el voo ruhmairsee

THEFT

My . . . has been stolen.
Mon/ma . . . a été volé(e)
mōn/ma . . . a aytay volay

Our room has been broken into.
Notre chambre a été cambriolée.
notr shōmbr a aytay kōmbree-olay

Our car has been broken into.
Notre voiture a été forcée et cambriolée.
notr vwatewr a aytay forsay ay kōmbree-olay

Can you cancel my credit cards for me?
Vous pouvez faire opposition à mes cartes de crédit ?
voo poovay fair oposeess-yōn a may kart duh kraydee

All my money has gone.
On a pris tout mon argent.
ōn a pree too mōn arjōn

It was on the table/in the wardrobe/in my pocket.
C'était sur la table/dans l'armoire/dans ma poche.
saytay sewr la tahbl/dōn larmwahr/dōn ma posh

I was only out for a couple of minutes.
J'étais sorti(e) pour quelques minutes à peine.
jaytay sortee poor kelkuh meenewt a pen

RESPONSES

Vous pouvez le/la décrire ?
voo poovay luh/la daykreer
Can you describe it?

Il y avait des objets de valeur ?
eel yavay day zobjay duh valur
Was there anything valuable?

137

TICKETS

Two tickets for the pool please.
Deux entrées pour la piscine, s'il vous plaît.
duh zōntray poor la peeseen seel voo play

Can I book two tickets for tomorrow night?
Je voudrais réserver deux places pour demain soir.
juh voodray rayzairvay duh plass poor duhmān swahr

I'd like two singles to ...
Je voudrais deux allers pour ...
juh voodray duh zalay poor

I'd like a return to ...
Je voudrais un aller-retour pour ...
juh voodray zān alay-ruhtoor poor

RESPONSES

Quand revenez-vous ?
kōn ruhvuhnay-voo
When are you coming back?

Première ou seconde ?
pruhm-yair oo suhgōnd
First class or second?

For coming back the same day.
Pour revenir le même jour.
poor ruhvuhneer luh mem joor

I'm/we're coming back in three days.
Je reviens/nous revenons dans trois jours.
juh ruhv-yān/noo ruhvuhnōn dōn trwa joor

I'd like to change this ticket and travel on Tuesday.
Je voudrais échanger ce ticket pour voyager mardi.
juh voodray ayshōnjay suh teekay poor vwī-ahjay mardee

138

TIME

(see also DAYS)

What's the time?
Quelle heure est-il ?
kel ur ay teel

Excuse me, could you tell me what time it is?
Excusez-moi, vous pouvez me donner l'heure ?
ex-kewzay-mwa voo poovay muh donnay lur

It's one o'clock.
Il est une heure.
eel ay ewn ur

It's ten past two.
Il est deux heures dix.
eel ay duh zur deess

It's a quarter past three.
Il est trois heures et quart.
eel ay trwa zur ay kar

It's twenty-five past four.
Il est quatre heures vingt-cinq.
eel ay katr ur vān-sānk

It's half past five.
Il est cinq heures et demie.
eel ay sānk ur ay duhmee

It's twenty to six.
Il est six heures moins vingt.
eel ay seess ur mwān vān

It's quarter to seven.
Il est sept heures moins le quart.
eel ay set ur mwān luh kar

It's five to eight.
Il est huit heures moins cinq.
eel ay weet ur mwan sank

It's just after nine.
Il est neuf heures passées.
eel ay nuhf ur pasay

It's just coming up to ten o'clock.
C'est presque dix heures.
say presk dee zur

It's around three o'clock.
Il est autour de trois heures.
eel ay ohtoor duh trwa zur

It's eleven o'clock exactly.
Il est onze heures exactement.
eel ay onz ur exaktuhmon

At eleven o'clock in the morning/at night.
A onze heures du matin/du soir.
a onz ur dew matan/dew swahr

At what time?
A quelle heure ?
a kel ur

It's getting very late.
Il se fait tard.
eel suh fay tar

Early in the morning.
Tôt le matin.
toh luh matan

In the early hours of the morning.
Aux aurores.
o zoror

140

Late at night.
Tard le soir.
tar luh swahr

Do we have time?
Nous avons le temps ?
noo zavōn luh tōm

There's plenty of time.
On a le temps.
ōn a luh tōm

Every two hours.
Toutes les deux heures.
toot lay duh zur

How long does it take?
Ça prend combien de temps ?
sa prōn kōmb-yān duh tōm

Half an hour.
Une demi-heure.
ewn duhmee-ur

Five minutes.
Cinq minutes.
sānk meenewt

Ages.
Des siècles.
day see-ekl

TOILETS

Can I use your toilet?
Je peux aller aux toilettes ?
juh puh alay o twalet

Where's the gents?
Où sont les toilettes pour hommes ?
oo son lay twalet poor om

Where are the ladies?
Où sont les toilettes pour dames ?
oo son lay twalet poor dam

I need to go for a pee.
Je dois aller faire pipi.
juh dwa alay fair peepee

She's in the toilet.
Elle est aux toilettes.
el ay o twalet

Can I have some toilet paper?
Je peux avoir du papier toilette ?
juh puh avwahr dew pap-yay twalet

It won't flush.
La chasse ne marche pas.
la shass nuh marsh pa

Could you go and see if he's/she's all right?
Vous pouvez aller voir si il/elle n'a pas de problème ?
voo poovay alay vwahr see eel/el na pa duh prob-lem

YOU'LL SEE

Dames.	**Hommes.**
dam	*hom*
Ladies.	Gents.

TRAINS

(see also TICKETS)

How much does the train to ... cost?
C'est combien un ticket pour ...?
say kōmb-yāṅ āṅ teekay poor

Is this train going to ...?
Est-ce que ce train va à ...?
eskuh suh trāṅ va a

Which platform is it for ...?
C'est quel quai pour ...?
say kel kay poor

Is this the right platform for ...?
C'est le bon quai pour ...?
say luh bōṅ kay poor

Do I have to change?
Faut-il que je change ?
fohteel kuh juh shōṅj

Do we change here for ...?
Nous devons changer ici pour... ?
noo duhvōṅ shōṅjay ee-see poor

What's this station called please?
Quelle est cette gare, s'il vous plaît ?
kel ay set gar seel voo play

When's the last train back to ...?
A quelle heure est le dernier train qui retourne à ...?
a kel ur ay luh dairn-yay trāṅ kee ruhtoorn a

> **Gare.**
> *gar*
> Station.

UNDERSTANDING PEOPLE

Pardon?, Sorry?
Pardon ? Excusez-moi ?
pardoñ ex-kewzay-mwa

Could you say that very slowly?
Vous pouvez répéter ça très lentement ?
voo poovay raypaytay sa tray loñtuhmoñ

Could you write that down?
Vous pouvez écrire ça ?
voo poovay aykreer sa

I don't understand.
Je ne comprends pas.
juh nuh kõmproñ pa

What did he say?
Qu'est-ce qu'il a dit ?
keskeel a dee

Could you interpret for me?
Vous pourriez traduire pour moi ?
voo pooree-ay tradweer poor mwa

Yes yes, I understand
Oui, oui je comprends
wee wee juh kõmproñ

Do you understand what I'm saying?
Vous comprenez ce que je dis ?
voo kõmpruhnay suh kuh juh dee

Oh, I see!
Ah d'accord !
a dakor

144

WEATHER

What's the weather like?
Quel temps fait-il ?
kel tōm fet-eel

It's a lovely day.
Il fait très beau.
eel fay tray boh

What a horrible day!
Quel temps horrible !
kel tōm oreebl

What's the forecast for tomorrow?
Quelle est la météo pour demain ?
kel ay la maytay-o poor duhmān

It's raining again.
Il pleut encore.
eel pluh ōnkor

It's going to rain.
Il va pleuvoir.
eel va pluhvwahr

It'll clear up later.
Ça va s'éclaircir plus tard.
sa va sayklairseer plew tar

It's very cold/hot.
Il fait très froid/chaud.
eel fay tray frwa/shoh

It's so incredibly hot.
Il fait une chaleur incroyable.
eel fay ewn shalur ānkrwi-yahbl

WINTER SPORTS

Can I have a ski-pass?
Je peux avoir un forfait ?
juh puh avwahr ān forfay

I'll meet you at the ski-tow.
On se retrouve au remonte-pente.
ōn suh ruhtroov o ruhmōnt-pont

I'm going to the beginners' slope.
Je vais sur la piste bleue.
juh vay sewr la peest bluh

I need to improve my turns.
Je dois améliorer mes virages.
juh dwa amaylee-oray may veerahj

Let's try a slalom.
Faisons un slalom.
fuh-zōn ān slalom

How much is a toboggan?
C'est combien pour un bob ?
say kōmb-yān poor ān bob

But you're an experienced skier.
Mais vous êtes un très bon skieur
may voo zet ān tray bōn skee-ur

Is this slope safe?
Cette piste est sans danger ?
set peest ay sōn dōnjay

Careful, it's icy!
Attention, c'est glacé !
atōnss-yōn say glassay

Dernière remontée à . . .	**Ski hors-piste interdit.**
dairn-yair ruhmōntay a	*skee or-peest āntairdee*
Last ski-lift at . . .	Skiing off-piste forbidden.

146

WISHES

If only I could ...
Si seulement je pouvais ...
see surlmōn juh poovay

I wish I could.
J'aimerais tellement pouvoir.
jemuhray telmōn poovwahr

Best wishes. (as written on card)
Amicalement.
ameekalmōn

Give him/her my best wishes.
Dîtes-lui bonjour de ma part.
deet-lwee bōnjoor duh ma par

He sends his best wishes.
Il envoie ses meilleures pensées.
eel ōnvwa say may-ur pōnsay

Have a good journey!
Bon voyage !
bōn vwi-ahj

Happy birthday!
Bon anniversaire !
bon aneevairsair

Happy Christmas!
Joyeux Noël !
jwi-yuh no-el

Happy New Year!
Bonne Année !
bon anay

And to you too.
Et à vous aussi.
ay a voo o-see

ENGLISH-FRENCH DICTIONARY

Cross-references in this dictionary are to the phrase and grammar sections in the preceding part of the book.

An asterisk against a verb indicates that this verb forms its past tense with **être**. For more information on this see the section called PAST TENSE.

A

a un, une; *see ARTICLES*
about (*approx*) environ
above au-dessus de
abroad à l'étranger
accelerator l'accélérateur *m*
accent l'accent *m*
accept accepter; *see
ACCEPTING*
accident l'accident *m*; *see
CAR ACCIDENTS*
accommodation le
logement; *see ROOMS*
accompany accompagner
account (*bank*) le compte
ache la douleur
adaptor (*for voltage*)
l'adaptateur *m*; (*plug*) la
prise multiple
address l'adresse *f*
address book le carnet
d'adresses
admission charge l'entrée *f*
adult l'adulte *m/f*
advance: in advance
d'avance
advertisement la publicité;
(*for job, flat etc*) l'annonce *f*
advise conseiller
aeroplane l'avion *m*
afraid: I'm afraid (of) j'ai
peur (de)
after après
afternoon l'après-midi *m*;
see DAYS
aftershave l'after-shave *m*
afterwards ensuite
again de nouveau
against contre
age l'âge *m*
agency l'agence *f*
agent le représentant; (*for
cars*) le concessionnaire

aggressive agressif
ago: a week ago il y a une
semaine
agree: I agree je suis
d'accord; *see AGREEING*
AIDS le SIDA
air l'air *m*
air-conditioning la
climatisation
air hostess l'hôtesse de
l'air *f*
airline la compagnie aérienne
airmail: by airmail par avion
airport l'aéroport *m*; *see
FLYING*
alarm l'alarme *f*
alarm clock le réveil
alcohol l'alcool *m*
alive vivant
all: all Frenchmen tous les
Français; **all French
women** toutes les
Françaises; **all the wine**
tout le vin; **all day** toute la
journée; **that's all** c'est
tout
allergic to allergique à
alleyway la ruelle
all-inclusive tout compris
allow permettre
allowed permis
all right: that's all right
d'accord
almost presque
alone seul
Alps les Alpes *fpl*
already déjà
also aussi
alternator l'alternateur *m*
although bien que
altogether en tout
always toujours
a.m.: at 7 a.m. à 7 heures du
matin

149

ambassador
l'ambassadeur *m*,
l'ambassadrice *f*

ambulance l'ambulance *f*

America l'Amérique *f*

American américain; *(man)*
l'Américain *m*; *(woman)*
l'Américaine *f*

among parmi

amp: 13-amp de 13 ampères

ancestor l'ancêtre *m*

anchor l'ancre *f*

ancient ancien

and et

angina l'angine de poitrine *f*

angry fâché

animal l'animal *m*

ankle la cheville

anniversary *(wedding)*
l'anniversaire de mariage *m*

annoying ennuyeux

anorak l'anorak *m*

another un/une autre;
another beer encore une
bière

answer la réponse; *(verb)*
répondre

ant la fourmi

antibiotic l'antibiotique *m*

antifreeze l'antigel *m*

antihistamine
l'antihistaminique *m*

antique: it's an antique
c'est un objet ancien

antique shop l'antiquaire *m*

antiseptic le désinfectant

**any: have you got any
bread/eggs?** avez-vous du
pain/des œufs ?; **I don't
have any** je n'en ai pas

anybody quelqu'un

anyway quand-même

apart from sauf

apartment l'appartement *m*

aperitif l'apéritif *m*

apologize s'excuser*

apology les excuses *fpl; see*
APOLOGIES

appalling épouvantable

appendicitis l'appendicite *f*

appetite l'appétit *m*

apple la pomme

apple pie la tarte aux
pommes

application form le
formulaire

appointment le rendez-vous

approve of approuver

apricot l'abricot *m*

April avril

architect l'architecte *m/f*

area la région

arm le bras

arrest arrêter

arrival l'arrivée *f*

arrive arriver*

art l'art *m*

art gallery le musée d'art

arthritis l'arthrite *f*

artificial artificiel

artist l'artiste *m/f*

as *(since)* comme; **as fast
as** aussi vite que; *see*
COMPARISONS

ashamed: to be ashamed
avoir honte

ashtray le cendrier

ask demander

asleep: to be asleep dormir

asparagus les asperges *fpl*

aspirin l'aspirine *f*

asthma l'asthme *m*

astonishing étonnant

at: at the station à la gare;
at Luc's chez Luc; **at 5
o'clock** à 5 heures

Atlantic l'Atlantique *m*

atmosphere *(in group,*

weather) l'atmosphère *f*
attractive séduisant
aubergine l'aubergine *f*
audience le public
August août
aunt la tante
Australia l'Australie *f*
Australian australien;
　(*man*) l'Australien *m*;
　(*women*) l'Australienne *f*
Austria l'Autriche *f*
Austrian autrichien
automatic automatique
autumn l'automne *m*
awake réveillé
awful affreux
axe la hache
axle l'essieu *m*

B

baby le bébé
baby-sitter le/la baby-sitter
bachelor le célibataire
back l'arrière *m*; (*of body*)
　le dos; **the back
　wheel/seat** la roue/le siège
　arrière; **to come back**
　revenir*; **to go back**
　rentrer*
backpack le sac à dos
bacon le lard maigre
bad mauvais
badly mal
bag le sac; (*suitcase*) la valise
bake cuire
baker's la boulangerie
balance (*verb: wheel*)
　équilibrer
balcony le balcon
bald chauve
ball (*large*) le ballon; (*small*)

la balle
ball-bearings le roulement à
　billes
ball-point pen le stylo à bille
banana la banane
bandage le pansement
bank la banque
bank manager le directeur
　d'agence
bar le bar
barbecue le barbecue
barber le coiffeur pour
　hommes
barmaid la serveuse
barman le barman
basement le sous-sol
basket le panier
bath le bain
bathing cap le bonnet de
　bain
bathroom la salle de bain
bath salts les sels de
　bain *mpl*
bathtub la baignoire
battery la pile; (*for car*) la
　batterie
be être; *see PAST TENSE*
beach la plage
beans les haricots *mpl*
beard la barbe
bearing (*in car etc*) la butée
beautiful beau *m*, belle *f*
because parce que
become devenir*
bed le lit; **single/double
　bed** lit à une place/à deux
　places; **to go to bed** aller*
　se coucher
bed and breakfast la
　chambre avec petit déjeuner
bed linen les draps de lit *mpl*
bedroom la chambre à
　coucher
bee l'abeille *f*

151

beef le bœuf
beer la bière
before avant
begin commencer
beginner le débutant, la débutante
beginning le début
behalf: on behalf of the company au nom de la société
behaviour le comportement
behind derrière
beige beige
Belgian belge; (*man/woman*) le/la Belge
Belgium la Belgique
believe croire
bell la cloche; (*for door, at reception*) la sonnette
belong to appartenir à
below sous
belt la ceinture
bend le virage
berth (*for yacht*) le mouillage; (*in ship*) la couchette
beside à côté de
best: the best le/la meilleur(e)
bet le pari; (*verb*) parier
better mieux
between entre
beyond au delà de
bicycle le vélo
bidet le bidet
big grand
bikini le bikini
bill la note; (*in restaurant*) l'addition *f*
binding (*ski*) la fixation
bird l'oiseau *m*
biro (*m*) le stylo à bille
birthday l'anniversaire; *see WISHES*

biscuit le biscuit
bit: a little bit un peu
bite la morsure; (*insect*) la piqûre
bitter amer
bitter lemon le bitter
black noir
black and white noir et blanc
blackberry la mûre
bladder la vessie
blanket la couverture
bleach (*for toilets etc*) l'eau de Javel *f*
bleed saigner
bless: bless you! à vos souhaits !
blind aveugle
blinds le store
blister l'ampoule *f*
blocked (*pipe etc*) bouché; (*road*) barré
blond blond
blood le sang
blood group le groupe sanguin
blouse le chemisier
blow-dry le brushing
blown (*fuse*) sauté
blue bleu
boarding pass la carte d'embarquement
boat le bateau
body le corps; (*car*) la carrosserie
boil bouillir
bolt le verrou; (*verb*) verrouiller
bomb la bombe
bone l'os; (*in fish*) l'arête *f*
bonnet (*car*) le capot
book le livre; (*verb*) réserver
bookshop la librairie

boot (*shoe*) la botte; (*car*) le coffre

border la frontière

boring ennuyeux

born: I was born in 1970 je suis né(e) en 1970

borrow emprunter

boss le patron, la patronne

both: both of them tous les deux

bottle la bouteille

bottle-opener l'ouvre-bouteille *m*

bottom le fond; (*of body*) le derrière; **at the bottom of** au fond de

bottom gear la première

bouncer le videur

bowl le bol

bowls (*game*) les boules *fpl*

bow tie le nœud papillon

box la boîte

box office le guichet

boy le garçon

boyfriend le petit ami

bra le soutien-gorge

bracelet le bracelet

brake le frein; (*verb*) freiner

brake drum le tambour de frein

brake fluid le liquide de freins

brake lining la garniture de frein

brake shoes la mâchoire de frein

branch (*tree*) la branche; (*company*) l'agence *f*

brand (*of product*) la marque

brandy le cognac

brave courageux

bread le pain;
   white/wholemeal bread le pain blanc/complet

break casser

break down (*car*) tomber* en panne

breakdown (*car*) la panne; (*nervous*) la dépression

breakdown service le service de dépannage

breakdown vehicle la dépanneuse

breakfast le petit déjeuner

breast le sein

breastfeed allaiter

breath l'haleine *f*

breathe respirer

breeze la brise

brick la brique

bridge (*over river etc*) le pont

brief court

briefcase la serviette

bright (*weather*) clair

brilliant (*idea etc*) brillant

bring apporter

Britain la Grande-Bretagne

British britannique

Brittany la Bretagne

brochure le prospectus

broke: I'm broke je suis fauché

broken cassé

broker (*insurance etc*) le courtier

brooch la broche

broom le balai

brother le frère

brother-in-law le beau-frère

brown marron

bruise le bleu

brush la brosse

Brussels sprouts les choux de Bruxelles *mpl*

bucket le seau

budget le budget

buffet meal le buffet repas

building le bâtiment

bulb (*light*) l'ampoule *f*
bull le taureau
bumper le pare-chocs
bungalow le bungalow
bunk beds les lits superposés *mpl*
buoy la bouée
burn la brûlure; (*verb*) brûler
bus l'autobus *m*; (*long distance*) le car
business les affaires *fpl*
business card la carte de visite
business trip le voyage d'affaires
bus station la gare routière
bus stop l'arrêt d'autobus *m*
busy occupé; (*street, bars*) animé
but mais
butcher's la boucherie
butter le beurre
butterfly le papillon
button le bouton
buy acheter
by par; **by car** en voiture

C

cabbage le chou
cabin (*ship*) la cabine
cable (*electrical*) le fil électrique
cable car le téléférique
café le café
cagoule le K-way
cake le gâteau
cake shop la pâtisserie
calculator la calculette
calendar le calendrier
call appeler

calm down se calmer*
Calor gas (*tm*) le butagaz
camera l'appareil-photo *m*; (*cinecamera*) la caméra
campbed le lit de camp
camping le camping
campsite le camping
camshaft l'arbre à cames *m*
can la boîte; **I/she can** je peux/elle peut; **can you ...?** pouvez-vous ...?; *see PERMISSION, PRESENT TENSE*
Canada le Canada
Canadian canadien; (*man*) le Canadien; (*woman*) la Canadienne
canal le canal
cancel annuler
candle la bougie
canoe le canoë
can opener l'ouvre-boîte *m*
cap (*hat*) la casquette
capital (*money*) le capital
capital (*city*) la capitale
captain le capitaine
car la voiture
caravan la caravane
caravan site le terrain de camping pour caravanes
carburettor le carburateur
card la carte; (*business*) la carte de visite
cardboard le carton
cardigan le gilet
car driver l'automobiliste *m/f*
care: to take care of s'occuper de*
careful prudent; **be careful!** faites attention !
car ferry le ferry
car hire la location de voitures

154

car keys les clés de la voiture
car park le parking
carpet la moquette
car rental la location de voitures
carriage le wagon
carrot la carotte
carry porter
carry-cot le porte-bébé
car wash le lavage de voitures
case (*suitcase*) la valise
cash: to pay cash payer comptant
cash desk la caisse
cash dispenser le distribanque
cassette la cassette
cassette player le lecteur de cassettes
castle le château
casual (*clothes*) décontracté
cat le chat
catastrophe la catastrophe
catch attraper; (*bus etc*) prendre
cathedral la cathédrale
Catholic catholique
cauliflower le chou-fleur
cause la cause
cave la grotte
ceiling le plafond
celebrate célébrer
celebration la célébration
cemetery le cimetière
centigrade centigrade; *see* CONVERSIONS
central heating le chauffage central
central station la gare centrale
centre le centre
century le siècle
certificate le certificat

chain la chaîne
chair la chaise
chairlift le télésiège
chairman le président
chairperson le président, la présidente
chalet le chalet
chambermaid la femme de chambre
chance: by chance par hasard
change (*small*) la monnaie; (*verb*) changer; (*clothes*) se changer*; **to change trains** changer de train
changeable (*weather*) variable
Channel la Manche
charge le prix
charter flight le charter
chassis le châssis
cheap bon marché
cheat (*somebody*) escroquer
check vérifier
check-in l'enregistrement des bagages *m*
cheers! à la vôtre !
cheese le fromage
chef le chef
chemist's la pharmacie
cheque le chèque
cheque book le chéquier
cheque card la carte d'identité bancaire
cherry la cerise
chest la poitrine
chestnut le marron
chewing gum le chewing-gum
chicken le poulet
chickenpox la varicelle
child l'enfant *m*
children's portion la portion pour enfant

chilled (*wine*) frais

chilly (*weather*) frais

chin le menton

chips les frites *fpl*

chocolate le chocolat; **milk chocolate** le chocolat au lait; **plain chocolate** le chocolat à croquer; **hot chocolate** le chocolat chaud

choke (*on car*) le starter

choose choisir

chop (*meat*) la côtelette

Christian name le prénom

Christmas Noël; *see* WISHES

church l'église *f*

cider le cidre

cigar le cigare

cigarette la cigarette

cigarette lighter le briquet; (*in car*) l'allume-cigare *m*

cinema le cinéma

circle le cercle; (*in cinema etc*) le balcon

citizen le citoyen, la citoyenne

city la ville

city centre le centre-ville

claim form le formulaire de réclamation

claret le bordeaux rouge

clarify clarifier

class la classe; **first class** la première; **second class** la seconde

classical music la musique classique

clean propre; (*verb*) nettoyer

cleansing cream la crème démaquillante

clear (*obvious*) clair

clever intelligent

client le client, la cliente

cliff la falaise

climate le climat

climber le grimpeur, la grimpeuse

climbing boots les chaussures de montagne

clips (*on ski*) les fixations; (*on boot*) les crochets

cloakroom (*coats*) le vestiaire

clock l'horloge *m*

close (*verb*) fermer

closed fermé

cloth le tissu

clothes les vêtements *mpl*

clothes peg la pince à linge

cloud le nuage

cloudy nuageux

club le club

clutch l'embrayage *m*

coach la car; (*train*) le wagon

coast la côte

coat le manteau; (*jacket*) la veste

coathanger le cintre

cockroach le cafard

cocktail le cocktail

cocoa le cacao

coconut la noix de coco

code (*dialling*) l'indicatif *m*; (*postal*) le code postal

coffee le café; **white coffee** le café crème

coin la pièce

Coke (*tm*) le coca-cola

cold froid; **it's cold** il fait froid; **I'm cold** j'ai froid; (*illness*) le rhume; **I've got a cold** je suis enrhumé

cold cream la crème de beauté

collar le col

colleague le/la collègue
collect (person, laundry)
  prendre
collection la collection;
  (mail) la levée
colour la couleur
colour film la pellicule
  couleur
comb le peigne
come venir*; **to come
  back** revenir*; **come in!**
  entrez !; *see PRESENT
  TENSE*
comfortable confortable
commercial commercial
Common Market le Marché
  Commun
compact disc le disque
  compact
company la société
company car la voiture de
  société
compartment le
  compartiment
compass la boussole
compensation la
  compensation
competitor le concurrent, la
  concurrente
complain se plaindre*
complaint (about hotel etc) la
  réclamation
complicated compliqué
compliment le compliment
component la pièce
comprehensive insurance
  l'assurance tous-risques *f*
compulsory obligatoire
computer l'ordinateur *m*
concert le concert
concrete le béton
condenser le condensateur
condition la condition;
  (state) l'état *m*

conditioner le baume après-
  shampooing
condom le préservatif
conductor (orchestra) le chef
  d'orchestre
conference la conférence
conference room la salle de
  conférence
confirm confirmer
confusing déroutant
congratulations!
  félicitations !
connecting rod la bielle
connection (travel) la
  correspondance
constipated constipé
consulate le consulat
contact contacter
contact lenses les lentilles
  de contact *fpl*
contacts (of person) les
  contacts *mpl*
contraceptive le
  contraceptif
contract le contrat
cook le cuisinier, la
  cuisinière; (verb) cuire;
  (meal) préparer
cooker la cuisinière
cooking utensils les
  ustensiles de cuisine *mpl*
cool frais *m*, fraîche *f*
coolant l'agent de
  refroidissement *m*
cooling system le système
  de refroidissement
cooperation la coopération
copy la copie
corkscrew le tire-bouchon
corner le coin
cornflakes les
  cornflakes *mpl*
correct correct
corridor le couloir

Corsica la Corse
cosmetics les produits de
beauté *mpl*
cost le prix; *(verb)* coûter
cot le lit d'enfant
cotton le coton
cotton wool le coton
hydrophile
couchette la couchette
cough la toux; *(verb)*
tousser
country le pays
countryside la campagne
couple *(man and woman)* le
couple; **a couple of ...**
quelques ...
course: of course bien sûr
cousin le cousin, la cousine
cow la vache
crab le crabe
crafts l'artisanat *m*
cramp la crampe
crankshaft le vilebrequin
crash la collision
crayfish *(fresh water)*
l'écrevisse *f*; *(sea)* la
langouste; *(small)* la
langoustine
cream la crème
crèche la garderie
credit le crédit
credit card la carte de crédit
credit note l'avoir *m*
crew l'équipage *m*
crisps les chips *fpl*
crockery la vaisselle
cross *(verb)* traverser
crossing *(by sea)* la
traversée; *(pedestrian)* le
passage clouté
crossroads le carrefour
crowd la foule
crowded bondé
cruise la croisière

crutches les béquilles *fpl*
cry pleurer
cucumber le concombre
cup la tasse
cupboard l'armoire *f*
currency la monnaie
current account le compte
courant
curry le curry
curtain le rideau
custom la coutume
customer le client, la cliente
customs la douane
cut couper
cutlery les couverts *mpl*
CV le CV
cycling le cyclisme
cyclist le/la cycliste
cylinder le cylindre
cylinder head gasket le
joint de culasse

D

dad le papa
damage endommager
damn! zut !
damp humide
dance danser; *see*
DANCING
danger le danger
dangerous dangereux
Danish danois
dare oser
dark sombre
dashboard le tableau de
bord
data processing le
traitement de données
date *(time)* la date;
(appointment) le rendez-
vous

daughter la fille
daughter-in-law la belle-fille
day le jour
dead mort
deaf sourd
deal l'affaire *f*; **it's a deal**
marché conclu !
dealer (*for cars etc*) le
concessionnaire
dear cher
death la mort
debt la dette
decaffeinated décaféiné
December décembre
decide décider
decision la décision
deck le pont
deck chair la chaise longue
deep profond
degree (*temperature*) le degré
delay le retard
deliberately exprès
delicious délicieux
demand exiger
Denmark le Danemark
dent la bosse
dentist le/la dentiste
dentures le dentier
deodorant le déodorant
department store le grand
magasin
departure le départ
depend: it depends ça
dépend
deposit (*as security*) la
caution; (*first payment*)
l'acompte *m*
depressed déprimé
dessert le dessert
develop développer
device l'appareil *m*
diabetic diabétique
dialect le dialecte
dialling code l'indicatif *m*

diamond le diamant
diarrhoea la diarrhée
diary l'agenda *m*
dictionary le dictionnaire
die mourir*
diesel (*fuel*) le gas-oil
diet le régime
difference la différence
different différent
difficult difficile
difficulty la difficulté
dining car le wagon-
restaurant
dining room la salle à
manger
dinner le dîner; **to have
dinner** dîner
dipped headlights les
codes *mpl*
dipstick la jauge
direct direct
direction le sens
director (*of company*) le
directeur, la directrice
directory enquiries les
renseignements *mpl*
dirty sale
disabled handicapé
disappear disparaître
disappointed déçu
disaster le désastre
disc brake le frein à disque
disco la discothèque
discount la remise
disease la maladie
disgusting dégoûtant
disinfectant le désinfectant
disk (*computer*) la disquette
distance la distance
distributor (*in car*) le delco
district (*in town*) le quartier
disturb déranger
dive plonger
divorced divorcé

do faire; **that'll do** ça va
bien
docks les docks *mpl*
doctor le médecin
document le document
dog le chien
doll la poupée
donkey l'âne *m*
door la porte
dormitory (*in hostel*) le
dortoir
double double
double bed le lit à deux
places
double room la chambre
pour deux personnes
Dover Douvres
down: down there là en bas
down payment l'acompte *m*
downstairs en bas
draught le courant d'air
dream le rêve
dress (*noun*) la robe; (*verb:
someone*) habiller; (*oneself*)
s'habiller*
dressing gown la robe de
chambre
drink la boisson; (*verb*)
boire
drinking water l'eau
potable *f*
drive conduire
driver le conducteur, la
conductrice
drive shaft l'arbre de
transmission *m*
driving licence le permis de
conduire
drop la goutte; (*verb*) laisser
tomber
drug (*narcotic*) la drogue
drunk ivre
drunken driving la conduite
sous état d'ivresse

dry sec *m*, sèche; (*verb*)
sécher
dry-cleaner le pressing
duck le canard
durex (*m*) le préservatif
during pendant
dustbin la poubelle
Dutch hollandais; **Dutch
woman** la Hollandaise
Dutchman le Hollandais
duty (*tax*) la taxe
duty-free hors taxes
duty-free shop la boutique
hors taxes
dynamo la dynamo

E

each chaque
ear l'oreille *f*
early tôt; (*too early*) en
avance
earrings les boucles
d'oreille *fpl*
earth la terre
east l'est *m*; **east of** à l'est
de
Easter Pâques
easy facile
eat manger
economy l'économie *f*
economy class la classe
économique
EEC CEE *f*
egg l'œuf *m*; **hard-boiled
egg** œuf dur; **boiled egg**
œuf à la coque
egg cup le coquetier
either ... or ... soit ... soit
...
elastic élastique
Elastoplast (*tm*) le

pansement adhésif
elbow le coude
electric électrique
electric blanket la
couverture électrique
electricity l'électricité *f*
else: something else autre
chose
elsewhere ailleurs
embarrassing gênant
embassy l'ambassade *f*
emergency l'urgence *f*
emergency exit la sortie de
secours
empty vide
end la fin
engaged (*toilet, phone*)
occupé; (*to be married*)
fiancé
engine le moteur; (*train*) la
locomotive
England l'Angleterre *f*
English anglais
Englishman l'Anglais *m*
English woman l'Anglaise *f*
enlargement
l'agrandissement *m*
enough assez; **that's
enough** ça suffit
enter entrer* dans
entertainment les
distractions *fpl*
entrance l'entrée *f*
envelope l'enveloppe *f*
epileptic épileptique
equipment l'équipement *m*
especially surtout;
especially for you
spécialement pour toi
estimate (*of costs*) le devis
Eurocheque
l'Eurochèque *m*
Eurocheque card la carte
Eurochèque

Europe l'Europe *f*
European européen
even (*number*) pair; **even
here/if** même ici/si; **even
faster** encore plus vite
evening le soir; **we had a
nice evening** nous avons
passé une bonne soirée; *see
HELLO*
every chaque; **every time**
chaque fois; **every day**
tous les jours
everyone tout le monde
everything tout
everywhere partout
exaggerate exagérer
example l'exemple *m*; **for
example** par exemple
excellent excellent
except sauf
excess baggage l'excédent
de bagages *m*
exchange échanger
exchange rate le cours du
change
exciting passionnant
excuse me pardon
executive le cadre
exhaust le pot
d'échappement
exhaust fumes les gaz
d'échappement
exhibition l'exposition *f*
exit la sortie
expenditure les dépenses *fpl*
expenses les frais *mpl*
expensive cher
experience l'expérience *f*
explain expliquer
export exporter
exposure (*photo*) la pose
exposure meter le
photomètre
express (*mail*) en exprès

extension lead la rallonge
eye l'œil *m*, *pl* les yeux
eyebrow le sourcil
eyeliner l'eye-liner *m*
eye shadow l'ombre à paupières *f*

F

face le visage
factory l'usine *f*
faint s'évanouir*
fair (*commercial, funfair*) la foire; (*adjective*) juste
fall tomber*
false faux
family la famille
famous célèbre
fan le ventilateur; (*supporter*) le/la fan
fan belt la courroie du ventilateur
far (away) loin
fare (*travel*) le prix (*du billet*)
farm la ferme
farmer l'agriculteur *m*
fashion la mode
fashionable à la mode
fast vite; (*adjective*) rapide
fat gros *m*, grosse *f*; (*noun*) le gras
father le père
father-in-law le beau-père
fault: it's my/his fault c'est de ma/sa faute
faulty défectueux
favourite préféré
fax le fax
fear la peur
February février
fed up: I'm fed up (with) j'en ai marre (de)

feel sentir; **I feel well/ill** je me sens bien/mal; **I feel like** j'ai envie de; *see* FEEL
feeling le sentiment; (*physical*) la sensation
felt-tip le stylo-feutre
feminist féministe
fence la barrière
ferry le ferry-boat; (*small*) le bac
fever la fièvre
few: few tourists peu de touristes; **a few** quelques-uns; **a few ...** quelques ...
fiancé(e) le fiancé, la fiancée
field le champ
fight la bagarre; (*verb*) se battre*
fill remplir
fillet le filet
filling (*tooth*) le plombage
film le film; (*for camera*) la pellicule
filter le filtre
financial financier
find trouver
fine l'amende *f*; (*adjective: good*) bon; (*weather*) beau; **fine!** très bien !
finger le doigt
fingernail l'ongle *m*
finish terminer
Finland la Finlande
Finnish finlandais
fire le feu; (*blaze*) l'incendie *f*
fire brigade les pompiers *mpl*
fire extinguisher l'extincteur *m*
fireworks le feu d'artifice
firm (*company*) la firme

162

first premier; *(firstly)* d'abord

first aid les premiers secours *mpl*

first class la première *(classe)*

first floor le premier

first name le prénom

fish le poisson

fishbone l'arête *f*

fishing la pêche

fishmonger's la poissonnerie

fit *(healthy)* en forme

fix *(arrange)* arranger; *(in position)* fixer

fizzy gazeux

flag le drapeau

flash le flash

flash cube le cube-flash

flat l'appartement *m*; *(adjective)* plat; *(tyre)* crevé; *(battery)* à plat

flat rate le montant forfaitaire

flavour l'arôme *m*

flea la puce

flight le vol

flirt flirter

floor *(of room)* le plancher; *(storey)* l'étage *m*

floppy disk le disque souple

florist's le fleuriste

flour la farine

flower la fleur

flu la grippe

fluently: to speak French fluently parler le français couramment

fly la mouche; *(verb)* voler

fog le brouillard

fog lights les antibrouillards *mpl*

folk music la musique folklorique

follow suivre

food la nourriture

food poisoning l'intoxication alimentaire *f*

foot le pied; **on foot** à pied

football le football

for pour

forbidden défendu

forehead le front

foreign étranger

foreigner l'étranger *m*, l'étrangère *f*

foreign exchange les devises *fpl*

forest la forêt

forget oublier

fork la fourchette; *(in road)* l'embranchement *m*

form *(document)* le formulaire

fortnight la quinzaine

fortunately heureusement

forward *(mail)* faire suivre

foundation cream le fond de teint

fountain la fontaine

four-star *(petrol)* le super

foyer le foyer

fracture la fracture

frame *(of picture)* le cadre

frames *(of glasses)* la monture

France la France

free libre; *(of charge)* gratuit

freezer le congélateur

freight le fret

French français

Frenchman le Français

French woman la Française

frequent fréquent

fresh frais *m*, fraîche *f*

Friday le vendredi

fridge le frigo

friend l'ami *m*, l'amie *f*

friendly amical

from: from Dover to Marseilles de Douvres à Marseille

front (*part*) l'avant *m*; **in front of** devant; **the front wheel/seat** la roue/le siège avant

frost le gel

frozen (*food*) surgelé

fruit les fruits *mpl*

fruit juice le jus de fruit

fry frire

frying pan la poêle

fuel le fuel

fuel tank le réservoir

full plein

full beam les pleins feux *mpl*

full board la pension complète

fun: to have fun s'amuser; **have fun!** amusez-vous bien !

funeral l'enterrement *m*

funnel (*for pouring*) l'entonnoir *m*

funny (*strange, amusing*) drôle

furious furieux

furniture les meubles *mpl*

further plus loin

fuse le fusible

future l'avenir *m*

G

game (*to play*) le jeu; (*meat*) le gibier

garage le garage; (*fuel*) la station-service

garden le jardin

garlic l'ail *m*

gas le gaz

gasket le joint d'étanchéité

gas permeable lenses les lentilles semi-rigides *fpl*

gastritis la gastrite

gauge la jauge

gay homosexuel

gear la vitesse

gearbox la boîte de vitesses

gear lever le levier de vitesse

generous généreux

gentleman le monsieur

gents (*toilet*) les toilettes pour hommes *fpl*

genuine authentique

German allemand; (*man*) l'Allemand *m*; (*woman*) l'Allemande *f*

German measles la rubéole

Germany l'Allemagne *f*

get obtenir; **can you tell me how to get to …?** pouvez-vous me dire comment aller à … ?; **it's getting cold** il commence à faire froid; **to get back** (*return*) rentrer*; **to get in** (*car*) monter* (*dans*); **to get off** descendre*; **to get out** (*car, train*) descendre*; dehors !; **get out!** dehors !

gift (*present*) le cadeau; (*talent*) le don

gin le gin

gin and tonic le gin-tonic

girl la jeune fille

girlfriend la petite amie

give donner; **to give back** rendre

glad content

glass le verre

glasses les lunettes *fpl*

glove compartment la boîte à gants

gloves les gants *mpl*
glue la colle
go aller*; **to go in** entrer*; **to go out** sortir*; **to go down** descendre*; **to go up** monter*; **to go through** traverser; **to go away** partir*; **go away!** allez-vous-en !; **it's all gone** c'est fini; *see PRESENT TENSE*
goat la chèvre
God Dieu *m*
gold l'or *m*
golf le golf
goodbye au revoir
good bon; **good!** bien!
good-looking beau *m*, belle *f*
goods les marchandises *fpl*
goose l'oie *f*
gorgeous magnifique
got: have you got ...? avez-vous ... ?
government le gouvernement
grammar la grammaire
grandfather le grand-père
grandmother la grand-mère
grapefruit le pamplemousse
grapes le raisin
grass l'herbe *f*
grateful reconnaissant
gravy la sauce au jus de viande
greasy gras
Greece la Grèce
Greek grec
green vert
green card la carte verte
greengrocer's le marchand de légumes
grey gris
grilled grillé

grocer's l'épicerie *f*
gross brut
ground floor le rez-de-chaussée
group le groupe
guarantee la garantie
guest l'invité *m*, l'invitée *f*
guesthouse la pension
guide le/la guide
guidebook le guide
guilty coupable
guitar la guitare
gun (*rifle*) le fusil; (*pistol*) le pistolet
gynaecologist le/la gynécologue

H

habit l'habitude *f*
hail (*ice*) la grêle
hair les cheveux *mpl*
hairbrush la brosse à cheveux
haircut la coupe de cheveux
hairdresser le coiffeur
hair dryer le sèche-cheveux
hair spray la laque
half la moitié; **half a litre/day** un demi-litre/une demi-journée; **half an hour** une demi-heure
half board la demi-pension
hall la salle; (*in house*) le hall
ham le jambon
hamburger le hamburger
hammer le marteau
hand la main
handbag le sac à main
handbrake le frein à main
handkerchief le mouchoir
handle la poignée

hand luggage les bagages à main *mpl*
handsome beau
hanger le cintre
hangover la gueule de bois
happen arriver*
happy heureux; *see WISHES*
harbour le port
hard dur
hard lenses les lentilles dures *fpl*
hardly à peine
hat le chapeau
hatchback la voiture à hayon
hate détester
have avoir; **I have to ...** je dois ...; *see PAST TENSE*
hay fever le rhume des foins
he il
head la tête
headache: I've got a headache j'ai mal à la tête
headlights les phares *mpl*
health la santé
healthy bon pour la santé; (*person*) en bonne santé
hear entendre
hearing aid l'audiophone *m*
heart le cœur
heart attack la crise cardiaque
heat la chaleur
heater le radiateur
heating le chauffage
heavy lourd
heel le talon
height (*person*) la taille; (*mountain*) l'altitude *f*
helicopter l'hélicoptère *m*
hello bonjour; *see ATTENTION, HELLO,*

TELEPHONING
helmet (*for motorbike*) le casque
help l'aide *f*; (*verb*) aider; **help!** au secours!
helpful (*person*) serviable; (*objects*) utile
her (*possessive*) son, sa, ses; *see POSSESSIVES*; (*object*) la; lui; elle; *see PRONOUNS*
herbs les fines herbes *fpl*
here ici; **here is/are** voilà; **here you are** (*offering*) voilà
hers le sien, la sienne; *see POSSESSIVES*
hiccups le hoquet
hide cacher
high haut
highway code le code de la route
hill la colline
hillwalking la randonnée de basse montagne
him le, lui; *see PRONOUNS*
hip la hanche
hire: for hire à louer
hire purchase l'achat à crédit *m*
his son, sa, ses; **it's his** c'est le sien, la sienne; *see POSSESSIVES*
history l'histoire *f*
hit frapper; (*hit record*) le tube
hitchhike faire du stop
hitchhiker l'autostoppeur *m*, l'autostoppeuse *f*
hitchhiking le stop
hobby le hobby
hold tenir
hole le trou

holiday les vacances *fpl*;
(*public*) le jour férié; **the
summer holidays** les
grandes vacances
Holland la Hollande
home: at home à la
maison; **to go home**
rentrer* à la maison
homemade fait maison
homesick: I'm homesick
mon pays me manque
honest honnête
honestly vraiment
honey le miel
honeymoon le voyage de
noces
hood (*of car*) la capote; (*of
coat etc*) la capuche
hoover (*tm*) l'aspirateur *m*
hope espérer; **I hope so**
j'espère; **I hope not**
j'espère que non
horn (*of car*) le klaxon
horrible horrible
horse le cheval
horse riding l'équitation *f*
hospital l'hôpital *m*
hospitality l'hospitalité *f*
hot chaud; (*to taste*) piquant
hotel l'hôtel *m*
hot-water bottle la
bouillotte
hour l'heure *f*
house la maison
housewife la femme au foyer
house wine le vin de la
maison
hovercraft l'aéroglisseur *m*
how? comment ?; **how are
you?** comment allez-
vous ?; **how are things?**
ça va ?; **how
many/much?** combien ?
hub le moyeu

hub cap l'enjoliveur *m*
humour l'humour *m*
hungry: I'm hungry j'ai faim
hurry se dépêcher*; **hurry
up!** dépêchez-vous !
hurt faire mal; **it hurts** ça
fait mal
husband le mari
hydraulic hydraulique
hydraulics l'hydraulique *f*

I

I je
ice la glace
ice axe le piolet
ice cream la glace
ice lolly l'esquimau *m*
idea l'idée *f*
idiot l'idiot *m*, l'idiote *f*
if si
ignition l'allumage *m*
ignition key la clé de contact
ignition lock le verrou
d'allumage
ill malade
immediately
immédiatement
import importer
important important
impossible impossible
improve améliorer
in dans; **in Nice** à Nice; **in
France/1945** en
France/1945; **in English**
en anglais; **is he in?** il est
là ?
inch le pouce; *see
CONVERSIONS*
included compris
incredible incroyable
independent indépendant

indicator (car) le clignotant
indigestion l'indigestion f
industrial industriel
industry l'industrie f
infection l'infection f
infectious contagieux
information le renseignement
information desk les renseignements mpl
injection la piqûre
injured blessé
injury la blessure
inner tube la chambre à air
innocent innocent
insect l'insecte m
insect bite la piqûre d'insecte
insect repellent la crème anti-insectes
inside à l'intérieur (de)
insomnia l'insomnie f
instant coffee le café soluble
instrument l'instrument m
insulating tape le ruban isolant
insurance l'assurance f
insurance policy la police d'assurance
intelligence l'intelligence f
intelligent intelligent
interest l'intérêt m
interested: to be interested in s'intéresser à
interesting intéressant
international international
interpreter l'interprète m/f
intersection le croisement
introduce présenter
invitation l'invitation f
invite inviter; see INVITING PEOPLE
invoice la facture
Ireland l'Irlande f

Irish irlandais
Irishman l'Irlandais
Irish woman l'Irlandaise
iron (metal) le fer; (for clothes) le fer à repasser; (verb) repasser
ironmonger's la quincaillerie
island l'île f
it ça; **it is ...** c'est ...
Italian italien; (man) l'Italien; (woman) l'Italienne
Italy l'Italie f
itch: it itches ça me démange

J

jack (car) le cric
jacket la veste
jam la confiture
January janvier
jaw la mâchoire
jazz le jazz
jealous jaloux
jeans le jean m
jellyfish la méduse
jeweller's la bijouterie
jewellery les bijoux mpl
Jewish juif, f juive
job le travail
jogging; to go jogging faire du jogging
joint (to smoke) le joint
joke la plaisanterie
journey le voyage; see WISHES
jug le pot
juice le jus
July juillet
jump sauter

jumper le pull
jump leads les cables de démarrage *mpl*
junction le croisement
June juin
just: just two deux seulement; **I've just arrived** je viens juste d'arriver; **just around the corner** juste au coin

K

keep garder
kerb le trottoir
kettle la bouilloire
key la clé
key ring le porte-clés
kidney le rein; *(food)* les rognons *mpl*
kill tuer
kilo le kilo; *see CONVERSIONS*
kilometre le kilomètre; *see CONVERSIONS*
kind aimable; *(type)* la sorte
king le roi
kiss le baiser; *(verb)* embrasser
kitchen la cuisine
knee le genou
knife le couteau
knit tricoter
knock frapper
knock over renverser
know savoir; *(person, place)* connaître; **I don't know** je ne sais pas
knowledge la connaissance

L

label l'étiquette *f*
ladder l'échelle *f*
ladies *(toilet)* les toilettes pour dames *fpl*
lady la dame
lager la bière blonde
lake le lac
lamb l'agneau *m*
lamp la lampe
lamppost le réverbère
land la terre; *(verb)* atterrir
landscape le paysage
lane *(alleyway)* la ruelle; *(on motorway)* la voie; *(small road in country)* le chemin
language la langue
language school l'école de langues *f*
large grand
last dernier; **last year** l'année dernière; **at last** enfin
late tard; *(delayed)* en retard
later plus tard
laugh rire
launderette le lavomatic
laundry *(to wash)* le linge sale; *(place)* la blanchisserie
law la loi
lawn la pelouse
lawyer l'avocat(e) *m/f*
laxative le laxatif
lazy paresseux
lead *(road)* mener
lead-free sans plomb
leaf la feuille
leaflet le dépliant
leak la fuite
learn apprendre
least: at least au moins
leather le cuir

169

leave laisser; (*go away*) partir*; (*forget*) oublier
left la gauche; **on the left (of)** à gauche (de)
left-hand drive la conduite à gauche
left-handed gaucher
left luggage la consigne
leg la jambe
lemon le citron
lemonade la limonade
lemon tea le thé citron
lend prêter
length la longueur
lens l'objectif *m*; (*in glasses*) le verre
less moins
lesson la leçon
let (*allow*) laisser
letter la lettre
letterbox la boîte à lettres
lettuce la laitue
level crossing le passage à niveau
lever le levier
library la bibliothèque
licence le permis; (*driving*) le permis de conduire
lid le couvercle
lie (*say untruth*) mentir
lie down s'étendre*
life la vie
life belt la bouée de sauvetage
life guard le surveillant de baignade
life jacket le gilet de sauvetage
lift (*elevator*) l'ascenseur *m*; **to give a lift to** emmener
lift pass le forfait
light (*in room*) la lumière; (*on car*) le phare; **have you got a light?** vous avez du

feu ?; (*adjective*) léger; **light blue** bleu clair; (*verb*) allumer
light bulb l'ampoule *f*
lighter le briquet
lighthouse le phare
light meter le photomètre
lightning l'éclair *m*
like aimer; **I would like** j'aimerais; (*as*) comme; *see* LIKES
lilo le matelas pneumatique
lip la lèvre
lipstick le rouge à lèvres
liqueur la liqueur
list la liste
listen (to) écouter
litre le litre; *see* CONVERSIONS
litter les ordures *fpl*
litterbin la poubelle
little petit; **a little bit (of)** un peu (de)
live vivre; (*in town etc*) habiter
liver le foie
living room le salon
lizard le lézard
load (*on lorry etc*) le chargement
loan le prêt
lobster le homard
lock la serrure; (*verb*) fermer à clé
locker le casier
lollipop la sucette
London Londres
lonely seul
long long *m*, longue *f*; **a long time** longtemps
long-distance call l'appel interurbain *m*
long-term à long terme
loo les toilettes *fpl*

look (*seem*) avoir l'air; **to
look** (*at*) regarder; **to
look like** ressembler à; **to
look for** chercher; **look
out!** attention !; **I looked
everywhere** j'ai cherché
partout
loose (*nut, handle*) lâche
lorry le camion
lose perdre
lost property office les
objets trouvés *mpl*
lot: a lot (of) beaucoup (de)
loud fort
lounge le salon
love l'amour *m*; (*verb*)
aimer; **to make love** faire
l'amour
lovely ravissant
low bas
luck la chance; **good luck!**
bonne chance !
luggage les bagages *mpl*
lukewarm tiède
lunch le déjeuner
lungs les poumons *mpl*
Luxembourg le
Luxembourg

M

macho macho
mad fou *m*, folle *f*; (*angry*)
furieux
magazine le magazine
maiden name le nom de
jeune fille
mail le courrier
main principal
main road la route principale
make faire; **made of silver**
en argent; **we'll never**

make it on n'y arrivera
jamais
make-up le maquillage
male chauvinist pig le
phallocrate
man l'homme *m*
manager le patron
many beaucoup; **many ...**
beaucoup de ...
map la carte; (*of town*) le
plan
March mars
margarine la margarine
market le marché
marmalade la confiture
d'oranges
marriage le mariage
married marié
mascara le mascara
mass (*church*) la messe
match (*light*) l'allumette *f*;
(*sport*) le match
material le tissu
matter: it doesn't matter ça
ne fait rien; **what's the
matter?** qu'est-ce qu'il y
a ?
mattress le matelas
May mai
maybe peut-être
mayonnaise la mayonnaise
me me; moi; **for me** pour
moi; **me too** moi aussi;
see PRONOUNS
meal le repas; **enjoy your
meal!** bon appétit !
mean (*verb*) signifier;
(*person: with money*) avare
measles la rougeole;
German measles la
rubéole
measurements les mesures
meat la viande
mechanic le mécanicien

171

medicine le médicament
Mediterranean la Méditerranée
medium *(steak)* à point
medium-sized moyen
meet rencontrer
meeting la réunion
meeting place le point de rendez-vous
melon le melon
member le membre
membership card la carte de membre
mend réparer
menu la carte; **set menu** le menu
mess la pagaille
message le message
metal le métal
meter le mètre; *see CONVERSIONS*
midday midi
middle le milieu
midnight minuit
mild *(taste, weather)* doux *m*, douce *f*
mile le mile; *see CONVERSIONS*
milk le lait
milkshake le milkshake
minced meat la viande hachée
mind: do you mind if I ...? ça vous dérange si je ... ?; **I don't mind** ça ne me dérange pas; **which one? – I don't mind** lequel? – ça m'est égal
mine le mien, la mienne; *see POSSESSIVES*
mineral water l'eau minérale *f*
minute la minute
mirror le miroir

Miss Mademoiselle, Mlle
miss *(train etc)* rater; **I miss you** tu me manques; **there's one missing** il en manque un
mistake l'erreur *f*
misunderstand mal comprendre
misunderstanding le malentendu
mix mélanger
mixture le mélange
model le modèle; *(fashion)* le mannequin
modern moderne
moisturizer la crème hydratante
Monday le lundi
money l'argent *m*
month le mois
monument le monument
mood l'humeur *f*
moon la lune
moped la mobylette
more plus; **no more ...** plus de ...; *see COMPARISONS*
morning le matin; *see SEE HELLO*
mosquito le moustique
most (of) la plupart (de); *see COMPARISONS*
mother la mère
mother-in-law la belle-mère
motorbike la moto
motorboat le bateau à moteur
motorist l'automobiliste *m/f*
motorway l'autoroute *f*
mountain la montagne
mountaineering l'alpinisme *m*
mouse la souris
moustache la moustache

mouth la bouche
move (*change position*) bouger; (*get something out of the way*) déplacer
Mr Monsieur, M
Mrs Madame, Mme
Ms Mme; Mlle
much beaucoup; **not much money** pas beaucoup d'argent
multi-storey carpark le parking à étages
mum la maman
muscle le muscle
museum le musée
mushrooms les champignons *mpl*
music la musique
mussels les moules *fpl*
must: I/she must je dois/elle doit; *see NECESSITY*
mustard la moutarde
my mon, ma, mes; *see POSSESSIVES*

N

nail (*in wall*) le clou; (*finger*) l'ongle *m*
nail clippers le coupe-ongles; (*bigger*) la pince à ongles
nailfile la lime à ongles
nail varnish le vernis à ongles
nail varnish remover le dissolvant
naked nu
name le nom; *see TALKING TO PEOPLE*
napkin la serviette
nappy la couche

nappy-liners les protège-couches *mpl*
narrow étroit
national national
nationality la nationalité
natural naturel
naturally naturellement
nature la nature
near près; **near here/the hotel** près d'ici/de l'hôtel; **the nearest ...** le/la ... le/la plus proche
nearly presque
neat (*drink*) pur; (*appearance*) soigné; (*room*) rangé
necessary nécessaire; *see NECESSITY*
neck le cou
necklace le collier
need: I need ... j'ai besoin de ...
needle l'aiguille *f*
negative (*film*) le négatif
negotiate négocier
negotiations les négociations *fpl*
neighbour le voisin, la voisine
neither ... nor ... ni ... ni ...
nephew le neveu
nervous nerveux
net (*for fishing, tennis*) le filet; **£500 net** 500 livres net
neurotic névrosé
neutral (*gear*) le point mort
never jamais
new nouveau *m*, nouvelle *f*; (*brand-new*) neuf *m*, neuve *f*
news les nouvelles *fpl*
newsagent le tabac-journaux

newspaper le journal
New Year le Nouvel An; *see WISHES*
next prochain; *(following)* suivant; **next year** l'année prochaine; **next to** à côté de
nice *(person)* sympathique; *(food)* bon; **it's nice here** c'est bien ici; **that's nice of you** c'est gentil
nickname le surnom
niece la nièce
night la nuit; *see HELLO*
nightclub la boîte de nuit
nightdress la chemise de nuit
nightmare le cauchemar
no non; **no ...** pas de ...; *see NEGATIVES*
nobody personne
noise le bruit
noisy bruyant
non-alcoholic sans alcool
nonsense! n'importe quoi !
non-smoking non-fumeurs
no-one personne
normal normal
north le nord; **north of** au nord de
Northern Ireland l'Irlande du Nord *f*
Norway la Norvège
Norwegian norvégien
nose le nez
nosey curieux
not pas; **I'm not ...** je ne suis pas ...; *see NEGATIVES*
note *(money)* le billet de banque
notebook le cahier
nothing rien
novel le roman

November novembre
now maintenant
nowhere nulle part
number *(room, phone)* le numéro; *(figure)* le chiffre
number plate la plaque minéralogique
nurse l'infirmière *f*; *(male)* l'infirmier *m*
nut *(to eat)* la noix; *(for bolt)* l'écrou *m*

O

obnoxious insupportable
obvious évident
occasion l'occasion *f*
occasionally à l'occasion
octane rating l'indice d'octane *m*
October octobre
octopus le poulpe
odd *(number)* impair; *(strange)* bizarre
of de; *see ARTICLES*
off *(lights)* éteint
offer offrir
office le bureau
official officiel; *(noun)* l'officiel *m*; *(government)* le fonctionnaire
often souvent
oil l'huile *f*
oil change la vidange
oil filter le filtre à huile
oil pressure la pression d'huile
ointment la pommade
OK d'accord; **I'm OK** ça va
old vieux *m*, vieille *f*; *see TALKING TO PEOPLE*
old-age pensioner le

retraité, la retraitée
old-fashioned démodé
old town la vieille ville
olive l'olive f
olive oil l'huile d'olive f
omelette l'omelette f
on sur; (*lights*) allumé; *see*
  DAYS
once une fois
one un m, une f *see*
  NUMBERS
onion l'oignon m
only seulement
open (*adjective*) ouvert;
  (*verb*) ouvrir
opening times les heures
  d'ouverture fpl
opera l'opéra m
operation l'opération f
operator (*telephone*)
  l'opératrice f
opportunity l'opportunité f
opposite le contraire;
  opposite the hotel en face
  de l'hôtel
optician l'opticien m,
  l'opticienne f
optimistic optimiste
or ou
orange l'orange f; (*colour*)
  orange
orange juice le jus d'orange
orchestra l'orchestre m
order commander; (*noun*)
  l'ordre m; (*restaurant*) la
  commande; **out of order**
  en panne
organization (*company etc*)
  l'organisation f
organize organiser
original (*first*) originel;
  (*play, idea etc*) original
other autre
otherwise sinon

our notre, nos; *see*
  POSSESSIVES
ours le/la nôtre; *see*
  POSSESSIVES
out (*lights*) éteint; **he's out**
  il est sorti; **we're out of**
  petrol nous n'avons plus
  d'essence
outside dehors
oven le four
over (*above*) au-dessus de;
  (*finished*) fini; **over there**
  là-bas
overdone trop cuit
overnight (*stay*) d'une nuit;
  (*travel*) de nuit
overtake doubler
owe devoir
own (*verb*) posséder; **my**
  own ... mon propre ...
owner le/la propriétaire
oyster l'huître f

P

pack faire ses bagages
package le paquet
package tour le voyage
  organisé
packed lunch le panier
  repas
packet (*of cigarettes etc*) le
  paquet
page la page; (*verb: person in*
  hotel etc) faire appeler
pain la douleur
painful douloureux
painkiller l'analgésique m
paint la peinture; (*verb*)
  peindre
paint brush le pinceau
painting le tableau

175

pair la paire
palace le palais
pancake la crêpe
panic la panique
panties le slip
paper le papier
papers (*passport, driving licence etc*) les papiers *mpl*
paraffin la paraffine
parcel le colis
pardon? comment ?
parents les parents *mpl*
park le parc; (*verb*) se garer*
parking lights les feux de position *mpl*
parking place la place de parking
partner (*personal, in business*) le/la partenaire
party (*celebration*) la fête; (*group*) le groupe; (*political*) le parti
pass (*mountain*) le col; (*verb*) passer
passenger le passager
passport le passeport
pasta les pâtes *fpl*
pâté le pâté
path le sentier
patience la patience
patient (*adjective*) patient
pavement le trottoir
pay payer
payment le paiement
payphone le téléphone public
peach la pêche
peanuts les cacahuètes *fpl*
pear la poire
peas les petits pois *mpl*
pedal la pédale
pedestrian le piéton, la piétonne

pedestrian crossing le passage clouté
pedestrian precinct la zone piétonne
pen le stylo
pencil le crayon
pencil sharpener le taille-crayon
penicillin la pénicilline
penis le pénis
penknife le canif
people les gens *mpl*
pepper (*spice*) le poivre; (*vegetable*) le poivron
per: per day par jour; **per cent** pour cent
perfect parfait
perfume le parfum
perhaps peut-être
period la période; (*woman's*) les règles *fpl*
perm la permanente
permanent permanent
permit l'autorisation *f*; (*verb*) permettre
person la personne
personal personnel
pessimistic pessimiste
petrol l'essence *f*
petrol gauge la jauge d'essence
petrol pump (*at garage*) la pompe d'essence; (*in car*) la pompe à essence
petrol station la station-service
petrol tank le réservoir d'essence
phone (*verb*) téléphoner (à)
phone book l'annuaire *m*
phone box la cabine téléphonique
phone card la carte Télécom
phone number le numéro

176

de téléphone

photocopy la photocopie

photograph la photographie; **to take a photograph of** photographier

photographer le/la photographe

phrase book le guide de conversation

pickpocket le pickpocket

pick up *(laundry, person from airport etc)* prendre

picnic le picnic

picture *(painting)* la peinture; *(photo)* la photo; *(drawing)* le dessin

pie *(fruit)* la tarte; *(meat)* la tourte

piece le morceau

pig le cochon

pigeon le pigeon

piles les hémorroïdes *fpl*

pile-up le carambolage

pill la pilule

pillarbox la boîte aux lettres

pillow l'oreiller *m*

pillow case la taie d'oreiller

pilot le pilote

pilot light la veilleuse

pin l'épingle *f*

pineapple l'ananas *m*

pink rose

pins and needles les fourmis

pipe le tuyau; *(to smoke)* la pipe

piston le piston

piston ring le segment de piston

pity: it's a pity c'est dommage

pizza la pizza

plain *(not patterned)* uni;

(yoghurt etc) nature

plane l'avion *m*

plant la plante

plastic le plastique

plastic bag le sac en plastique

plate l'assiette *f*

platform *(station)* le quai

play *(theatre)* la pièce de théâtre; *(verb)* jouer

pleasant agréable

please s'il vous plaît

pleased content; **pleased to meet you!** enchanté !

plenty: plenty of beaucoup de; **that's plenty** ça suffit

pliers la pince

plug *(electrical)* la prise; *(in sink)* la bonde

plum la prune

plumber le plombier

p.m.: 4 p.m. 4 heures de l'après-midi; **10 p.m.** 10 heures du soir

pneumonia la pneumonie

pocket la poche

points *(in car)* les contacts *mpl*

poison le poison

poisonous toxique

Poland la Pologne

police la police

policeman l'agent *m*

police station le commissariat

polite poli

political politique

politics la politique

polluted pollué

pond l'étang *m*

pool *(swimming)* la piscine

poor pauvre; *(performance, quality)* mauvais

pop music la musique pop

177

pop star la star pop
popular populaire
pork le porc
port (*drink*) le porto
porter (*hotel*) le portier
Portugal le Portugal
Portuguese portugais
possibility la possibilité
possible possible; *see*
  POSSIBILITIES
post (*letter*) poster
postcard la carte postale
poster (*for room*) le poster;
  (*in street*) l'affiche *f*
poste restante la poste
  restante
postman le facteur
post office la poste
potato la pomme de terre
poultry la volaille
pound la livre; *see*
  CONVERSIONS
powder (*for face etc*) la
  poudre *f*
power cut la coupure de
  courant
powerful puissant
practical pratique
**practise: I want to practise
  my French** je veux
  pratiquer mon français
pram le landau
prawn la crevette
prefer préférer
pregnant enceinte
prepare préparer
prescription l'ordonnance *f*
present (*gift*) le cadeau; **at
  present** à présent
president (*of country*) le
  président, la présidente
press (*newspapers*) la presse
pretty joli; **pretty good**
  pas mal; **pretty**

expensive assez cher
price le prix
price list la liste des prix
priest le prêtre
prince le prince
princess la princesse
print (*photo*) l'épreuve *f*;
  (*painting*) la reproduction
printed matter l'imprimé *m*
prison la prison
private privé
probably probablement
problem le problème
procedure la procédure
produce produire
product le produit
profit le profit
program(me) le programme
prohibited interdit
promise la promesse;
  (*verb*) promettre
pronounce prononcer
pronunciation la
  prononciation
propeller shaft (*of boat*)
  l'hélice *f*
prostitute la prostituée
protect protéger
protection factor l'indice de
  protection *m*
Protestant protestant;
  Protestant church le
  temple
proud fier
public public
publicity la publicité
pudding (*dessert*) le dessert
pull tirer
pump la pompe
puncture la crevaison
pure (*gold, silk etc*) pur
purple violet
purse le porte-monnaie
push pousser

pushchair la poussette
put mettre
pyjamas le pyjama

Q

quality la qualité
quarter le quart
quay le quai
queen la reine
question la question
queue la queue; (*verb*) faire
la queue
quick rapide
quickly vite
quiet tranquille; **quiet!**
silence !
quilt le duvet
quite assez
quote (*from author*) la
citation; (*price*) la cotation

R

rabbit le lapin
race (*sport*) la course
radiator le radiateur
radio la radio
rail: by rail en train; (*send*)
par train
railway le chemin de fer
rain la pluie; (*verb*)
pleuvoir; **it's raining** il
pleut
rainbow l'arc-en-ciel *m*
raincoat l'imperméable *m*
rape le viol
rare rare; (*steak*) bleu
rarely rarement
rash (*on skin*) l'éruption *f*

raspberry la framboise
rat le rat
rate (*of exchange*) le taux
rather plutôt; **I'd rather ...**
je préférerais ...
raw cru
razor le rasoir
razor blade la lame de rasoir
read lire
ready prêt
really vraiment
rear lights les feux
arrière *mpl*
rearview mirror le
rétroviseur
rear wheels les roues
arrière *fpl*
reason la raison
reasonable (*price, person*)
raisonnable
receipt le reçu
receive recevoir
recently récemment
reception (*hotel*) la réception
reception desk la réception
receptionist le/la
réceptionniste
recipe la recette
recognize reconnaître
recommend recommander
record le disque; (*sport etc*)
le record
record player
l'électrophone *m*
record shop le disquaire
red rouge
red-headed roux *m*, rousse *f*
red light district le quartier
des prostituées
reduction la réduction
refrigerator le réfrigérateur
refund rembourser
registered mail le courrier
recommandé

registration number le numéro d'immatriculation

regular régulier

regulations le règlement

relax se détendre*

reliable (*car, person*) sûr

religion la religion

remember se souvenir de*; **I remember** je m'en souviens

rent le loyer; (*verb*) louer; *see* RENTALS

repair réparer

repeat répéter

reply la réponse

report le rapport

representative (*of company*) le représentant, la représentante

reservation la réservation

reserve réserver

responsibility la responsabilité

responsible responsable

rest (*remainder*) le reste; (*sleep*) le repos; **to take a rest** se reposer*

restaurant le restaurant

return ticket l'aller retour *m*

rev counter le compte-tour

reverse (*gear*) la marche arrière

rheumatism les rhumatismes *mpl*

rib la côte

rice le riz

rich riche; (*food*) lourd

ridiculous ridicule

right (*side*) la droite; **on the right (of)** à droite (de); (*correct*) juste; *see* AGREEING WITH PEOPLE

right-hand drive la conduite à droite

right of way la priorité

ring (*on finger*) la bague; (*phone*) téléphoner (à)

ring road le périphérique

ripe mûr

river la rivière; (*flowing into sea: Seine etc*) le fleuve

road la route; (*in town*) la rue

roadsign le panneau de signalisation

roadworks les travaux *mpl*

rock le rocher; (*music*) le rock

rock climbing la varappe

roll (*bread*) le petit pain

roof le toit

roof rack la galerie

room la chambre

room service le service en chambre

rope la corde

rose la rose

rosé wine le rosé

rotten pourri; (*lousy*) mauvais

round (*circular*) rond; *see* DRINKS

roundabout le rond-point

route l'itinéraire *m*

rowing boat le bateau à rames

rubber le caoutchouc; (*eraser*) la gomme

rubber band l'élastique *m*

rubbish les ordures *fpl*; **rubbish!** n'importe quoi !; **these are rubbish** ça ne vaut rien

rucksack le sac à dos

rude grossier

rug le tapis

ruins les ruines *fpl*

rum le rhum
run courir; *(buses)* passer*;
(trains: leave) partir*
rush hour les heures de
pointe *fpl*
rust la rouille

S

sad triste
saddle la selle
safe en sécurité
safety pin l'épingle de
nourrice *f*
sailboard la planche à voile
sailing la voile
sailing boat le bateau à voile
salad la salade
salad dressing la
vinaigrette
salary le salaire
sale la vente; *(reduced price)*
les soldes *mpl* ; **for sale** à
vendre
salesman *(shop)* le
vendeur; *(representative)* le
représentant
salmon le saumon
salt le sel
salty salé
same: the same ... le/la
même ...
sample l'échantillon *m*
sand le sable
sand dunes les dunes *fpl*
sandwich le sandwich
sanitary towel la serviette
hygiénique
Saturday le samedi
sauce la sauce
saucepan la casserole
saucer la soucoupe

sauna le sauna
sausage la saucisse
savoury salé
say dire
scarf *(neck)* l'écharpe *f*;
(head) le foulard
scenery le paysage
schedule le programme;
behind schedule en
retard; **on schedule** à
l'heure; *(with project etc)*
dans les temps
school l'école *f*
science la science
scientist le/la scientifique
scissors les ciseaux *mpl*
Scot l'Écossais *m*,
l'Ecossaise *f*
Scotland l'Écosse *f*
Scottish écossais
scrambled eggs les œufs
brouillés *mpl*
scream crier
screw la vis
screwdriver le tournevis
sea la mer
seafood les fruits de
mer *mpl*
seagull la mouette
search chercher
seasick: I feel seasick j'ai
le mal de mer
seaside: at the seaside au
bord de la mer
season la saison; **in the
high season** en haute
saison
seasoning l'assaisonnement
seat le siège; *(place)* la place
seat belt la ceinture de
sécurité
seaweed les algues *fpl*
second deuxième; *(in time)*
la seconde

second class la seconde
second-hand d'occasion
secret secret
security (*in hotel etc*) la sécurité
see voir
seldom rarement
selection (*of wines etc*) le choix
self-service le self-service
sell vendre
sellotape (*tm*) le scotch (*tm*)
send envoyer
sender l'expéditeur *m*
sensible raisonnable
sensitive sensible
separate séparé
separately séparément
September septembre
serious sérieux
serve servir
service le service
service charge le service
service station la station-service
serviette la serviette
several plusieurs
sew coudre
sex le sexe
sexist sexiste
sexy sexy
shade l'ombre *f*
shampoo le shampoing
share partager
shares (*financial*) les actions *fpl*
shark le requin
sharp (*knife*) coupant; (*taste*) âpre
shave se raser*
shaving brush le blaireau
shaving foam la mousse à raser
she elle

sheep le mouton
sheet le drap
shell (*egg*) la coquille; (*sea*) le coquillage
shellfish les crustacés *mpl*
ship le bateau
shirt la chemise
shock le choc
shock-absorber l'amortisseur *m*
shocking scandaleux
shoe la chaussure
shoe laces les lacets *mpl*
shoe polish le cirage
shoe repairer le cordonnier
shop le magasin
shop assistant le vendeur, la vendeuse
shopping le shopping; **to go shopping** faire du shopping
shopping bag le cabas
shopping centre le centre commercial
shop window la vitrine
shore le rivage
short court
short circuit le court-circuit
shortcut le raccourci
shorts les shorts *mpl*
shortsighted myope
short-term à court terme
shoulder l'épaule *f*
shout crier
show montrer
shower la douche; (*rain*) l'averse *f*
shut (*adjective*) fermé; (*verb*) fermer
shutter (*photo*) l'obturateur *m*
shutters (*window*) les volets *mpl*
shy timide

sick: I feel sick je me sens mal; **I'm going to be sick** j'ai envie de vomir

side le côté

sidelights les feux de position *mpl*

sign le signe; (*verb: name*) signer

signature la signature

silence le silence

silencer le silencieux

silk la soie

silver l'argent *m*

silver foil le papier d'aluminium

similar pareil

simple simple

since (*time*) depuis (que); **since I've been here** depuis que je suis ici

sincere sincère

sing chanter

single (*unmarried*) célibataire

single room la chambre pour une personne

single ticket l'aller simple *m*

sink (*go under*) couler; (*in kitchen*) l'évier *m*

sister la sœur

sister-in-law la belle-sœur

sit down s'asseoir*

site le site; (*camping etc*) le camping

situation la situation

size la taille

ski le ski; (*verb*) skier; *see WINTER SPORTS*

ski boots les chaussures de ski *fpl*

skid déraper

skiing le ski

ski instructor le moniteur/la monitrice de ski

ski-jump le saut à ski;

(*structure*) le tremplin

ski-lift le remonte-pente

skin la peau

skin cleanser le démaquillant

skin-diving la plongée sous-marine

skinny maigre

ski-pants les fuseaux de ski *mpl*

ski-pass le forfait de ski

ski pole le bâton de ski

skirt la jupe

ski run la piste de ski

ski slope la piste de ski

skull le crâne

sky le ciel

sleep dormir

sleeper le wagon-lit

sleeping bag le sac de couchage

sleeping pill le somnifère

sleepy: I'm sleepy j'ai sommeil

slice la tranche

slide (*phot*) la diapositive

slim mince

slippers les pantoufles *fpl*

slippery glissant

slow lent

slowly lentement

small petit

small change la monnaie

smell l'odeur *f*; (*verb*) sentir

smile le sourire; (*verb*) sourire

smoke la fumée; (*verb*) fumer; *see SMOKING*

smoking (*compartment*) fumeurs

smooth (*skin*) doux; (*texture*) lisse; (*drink*) mœlleux

snack le casse-croûte
snail l'escargot *m*
snake le serpent
sneeze éternuer
snore ronfler
snow la neige; (*verb*) neiger
so: so funny/small si drôle/petit
soaking solution la solution de trempage
soap le savon
sober sobre
soccer le football
society la société
sock la chaussette
socket la prise
sofa le canapé
soft doux *m*, douce *f*
soft drink la boisson non-alcoolisée
soft lenses les lentilles souples *fpl*
software le logiciel
sole (*of shoe*) la semelle; (*of foot*) la plante
solution la solution
some: some milk/beer/buttons du lait/de la bière/des boutons
somebody quelqu'un
something quelque chose
sometimes parfois
somewhere quelque part
son le fils
song la chanson
son-in-law le beau-fils
soon bientôt
sore: I've got a sore throat j'ai mal à la gorge
sorry excusez-moi; **I'm sorry** je suis désolé; *see* APOLOGIES
soup le potage
sour acide

south le sud; **south of** au sud de
souvenir le souvenir
spade la pelle
Spain l'Espagne *f*
Spanish espagnol
spanner la clé anglaise
spare parts les pièces de rechange *fpl*
spare tyre la roue de secours
spark plug la bougie
speak parler; **do you speak ...?** parlez-vous ...?
specialist le/la spécialiste
speciality la spécialité
spectacle case l'étui à lunettes
spectacles les lunettes *f*
speed la vitesse
speed limit la limitation de vitesse
speedometer le compteur
spell écrire; (*speaking*) épeler; *see* ALPHABET
spend dépenser
spice l'épice *f*
spider l'araignée *f*
spinach les épinards *mpl*
splendid splendide
spoke le rayon
sponge l'éponge *f*
spoon la cuiller
sport le sport
spot (*on skin*) le bouton
sprain: I've sprained my ankle je me suis foulé la cheville
spring (*season*) le printemps; (*in seat etc*) le ressort
square (*in town*) la place
stain la tache
stairs l'escalier *m*
stamp le timbre

184

stand se tenir*; **to stand up** se lever*; *see* DISLIKES

star l'étoile *f*

start (*verb intransitive*) commencer; **the car won't start** la voiture ne démarre pas

starter (*car*) le démarreur; (*food*) l'entrée *f*

state l'état *m*

statement (*bank*) le relevé bancaire

station la gare

stationer's la papeterie

stay le séjour; (*remain*) rester*; (*in hotel etc*) loger

steak le steak

steal voler

steep raide

steering la direction

steering wheel le volant

stepfather le beau-père

stepmother la belle-mère

steward le steward

stewardess l'hôtesse de l'air *f*

sticky collant

still (*adverb*) encore; **keep still** ne bougez pas

sting piquer

Stock Exchange la Bourse

stockings les bas *mpl*

stomach le ventre

stomach ache les maux d'estomac *mpl*

stone la pierre

stop (*bus-*) l'arrêt *m*; (*verb*) s'arrêter*; (*someone, something*) arrêter; **stop!** arrêtez !

store (*put in storage*) entreposer; (*shop*) le magasin

storey l'étage *m*

storm la tempête

story l'histoire *f*

straight ahead tout droit

strange (*odd*) bizarre

stranger l'étranger *m*, l'étrangère *f*

strawberry la fraise

stream le ruisseau

street la rue

stress le stress

strike la grève

string la ficelle

stroke (*attack*) l'attaque *f*

strong fort

stuck: it's stuck c'est coincé

student l'étudiant *m*, l'étudiante *f*

stupid stupide

suburbs la banlieue

success le succès

successful (*person*) prospère; (*trip*) fructueux

suddenly tout d'un coup

suede le daim

sugar le sucre

suggest suggérer; *see* SUGGESTIONS

suit le complet; **it suits you** ça vous va bien

suitable adéquat

suitcase la valise

summer l'été *m*

sump le carter

sun le soleil

sunbathe se faire* bronzer

sunblock l'écran total

sunburn le coup de soleil

Sunday le dimanche

sunglasses les lunettes de soleil *fpl*

sunny: it's sunny il fait du soleil

sunrise le lever du soleil

sunset le coucher de soleil
sunshine le soleil
sunstroke l'insolation *f*
suntan le bronzage
suntan lotion le lait solaire
suntan oil l'huile solaire *f*
supermarket le supermarché
supper le dîner
supplement le supplément
supply fournir
sure sûr
surname le nom de famille
surprise la surprise
surprising surprenant
suspension (*car*) la suspension
swallow avaler
sweat transpirer
sweater le pullover
Sweden la Suède
Swedish suédois
sweet le bonbon
sweet (*to taste*) doux *m*, douce *f*
swim nager
swimming la natation; **to go swimming** aller se baigner
swimming costume le maillot de bain
swimming pool la piscine
swimming trunks le maillot de bain
Swiss suisse
switch l'interrupteur *m*
switch off (*light, television*) éteindre; (*engine*) arrêter
switch on (*light, television*) allumer; (*engine*) mettre en marche
Switzerland la Suisse
swollen enflé
synagogue la synagogue
synthetic synthétique

T

table la table
tablecloth la nappe
tablet le comprimé
table tennis le ping-pong
tail la queue
tailback le bouchon
take prendre; **to take away** (*remove*) enlever; (*food*) à emporter; **to take off** (*plane*) décoller; (*clothes*) enlever
talc le talc
talk parler
tall grand
tampon le tampon
tan (*colour*) le bronzage
tank le réservoir
tap le robinet
tape (*cassette*) la bande magnétique; (*sticky*) le scotch (*tm*)
tape recorder le magnétophone
target (*objective*) le but
tart la tarte
taste le goût; (*verb: try*) goûter
tax l'impôt *m*
taxi le taxi; *see TAXIS*
taxi driver le chauffeur de taxi
taxi rank la station de taxi
tea le thé
tea bag le sachet de thé
teach enseigner; **will you teach me some French?** apprenez-moi un peu de français
teacher le/la professeur
team l'équipe *f*
teapot la théière
tea towel le torchon à

vaisselle
technical technique
teenager l'adolescent *m*, l'adolescente *f*
telegram le télégramme
telephone le téléphone
telephone box la cabine téléphonique
telephone directory le bottin
television la télévision; **on television** à la télévision; **to watch television** regarder la télévision
telex le télex
temperature la température
temporary temporaire
tennis le tennis
tent la tente
tent peg le piquet
terrible épouvantable
terrific fantastique
test tester
than que; *see* COMPARISONS
thank remercier; **thank you** merci; *see* THANKS
that (*adjective*) ce, cette; (*pronoun*) ça, cela; **I think that ...** je pense que ...; **that one** celui-là, celle-là; *see* REFERRING TO THINGS
the le, la, les; *see* ARTICLES
theatre le théâtre
their leur; *see* POSSESSIVES
theirs le/la leur; *see* POSSESSIVES
them les; leur; eux; *see* PRONOUNS
then alors
there là; **there is/are ...** il

y a ...; **is/are there ...?** est-ce qu'il y a ... ?
thermometer le thermomètre
thermos flask le thermos
thermostat le thermostat
these (*adjective*) ces; (*pronoun*) ceux-ci, celles-ci; *see* REFERRING TO THINGS
they ils *m*, elles *f*; *see* PRONOUNS
thick épais
thief le voleur, la voleuse
thigh la cuisse
thin mince
thing la chose
think penser
third party (*insurance*) l'assurance au tiers
thirsty: I'm thirsty j'ai soif
this (*adjective*) ce, cette; (*pronoun*) ceci; **this one** celui-ci, celle-ci; *see* REFERRING TO THINGS
those (*adjective*) ces; (*pronoun*) ceux-là, celles-là; *see* REFERRING TO THINGS
thread le fil
throat la gorge
throat lozenges les pastilles pour la gorge *fpl*
through par
throw lancer; **to throw away** jeter
thumb le pouce
thunder le tonnerre
thunderstorm l'orage *m*
Thursday le jeudi
ticket le ticket; (*train, plane*) le billet
ticket office le guichet

187

tide la marée
tie la cravate
tight étroit
tights les collants *mpl*
time le temps; **two/three times** deux/trois fois; **next time** la prochaine fois; **on time** à l'heure; **what time is it?** quelle heure est-il ?; *see TIME*
timetable l'horaire *m*
tin opener l'ouvre-boîte *m*
tip le pourboire
tired fatigué
tiring fatigant
tissues les kleenex *(tm) mpl*
to: I'm going to Paris/Switzerland je vais à Paris/en Suisse
toast *(bread)* le toast
tobacco le tabac
today aujourd'hui
toe l'orteil *m*
together ensemble
toilet les toilettes *fpl*
toilet paper le papier hygiénique
tomato la tomate
tomorrow demain; *see DAYS*
tongue la langue
tonight ce soir
tonsillitis l'angine *f*
tonsils les amygdales *fpl*
too *(also)* aussi; **too hot** trop chaud; **not too much** pas trop
tool l'outil *m*
tooth la dent
toothache le mal de dents
toothbrush la brosse à dents
toothpaste le dentifrice
top: at the top en haut
torch la lampe de poche

touch toucher
tough *(meat)* dur; *(task, problem)* difficile; **tough luck!** manque de pot !
tour l'excursion *f*; *(of chateau etc)* la visite
tourist le/la touriste
tow remorquer
towel la serviette de bain
tower la tour
tow line le cable de remorquage
town la ville
town hall la mairie
toy le jouet
tracksuit le survêtement
trade union le syndicat
tradition la tradition
traditional traditionnel
traffic la circulation
traffic jam l'embouteillage *m*
traffic lights les feux de signalisation *mpl*
traffic warden le contractuel, la contractuelle
trailer *(behind car)* la remorque
train le train
trainers les tennis *fpl*
transformer le transformateur
transistor *(radio)* le transistor
translate traduire
translation la traduction
translator le traducteur, la traductrice
travel voyager
travel agent's l'agence de voyages *f*
traveller's cheque le chèque de voyage
tray le plateau
tree l'arbre *m*

tremendous formidable
trip (*outing*) l'excursion *f*;
  (*journey*) le voyage
trolley le chariot
trouble les ennuis *mpl*
trousers le pantalon
true vrai
truth la vérité
try essayer; **to try on**
  essayer
T-shirt le T-shirt
tube (*tyre*) la chambre à air
Tuesday le mardi
tuna fish le thon
tunnel le tunnel
turkey la dinde
Turkey la Turquie
turn tourner; **to turn off**
  (*driving*) tourner
tweezers la pince à épiler
twice deux fois
twin beds les lits
  jumeaux *mpl*
twins les jumeaux *mpl*
two-star (*petrol*) l'ordinaire *f*
typewriter la machine à
  écrire
typical typique
tyre le pneu
tyre lever le démonte-pneu
tyre pressure la pression des
  pneus

U

ugly laid
umbrella le parapluie
uncle l'oncle *m*
under sous
underdone mal cuit
underground le métro
underneath dessous ;

underneath ... sous ...
underpants le slip
understand comprendre;
  *see UNDERSTANDING
  PEOPLE*
underwear les sous-
  vêtements *mpl*
unemployed au chômage
unfortunately
  malheureusement
United States les Etats-
  Unis *mpl*
university l'université *f*
unleaded sans plomb
unpack défaire sa valise
unpleasant désagréable
until jusqu'à; **until I ...**
  jusqu'à ce que je ...
unusual inhabituel
up: up there là-haut
upside down à l'envers
upstairs en haut
urgent urgent
us nous
use utiliser
useful utile
usual habituel
usually d'habitude
U-turn le demi-tour

V

vacancy (*room*) la chambre
  libre
vacation les vacances *fpl*
vaccination le vaccin
vacuum cleaner
  l'aspirateur *m*
vagina le vagin
valid valable
valley la vallée
valuable valable

valve la valve
van la camionnette
vanilla la vanille
vase le vase
VAT la TVA
VD la maladie vénérienne
veal le veau
vegetables les légumes *mpl*
vegetarian végétarien
vehicle le véhicule
very très; **very much** beaucoup
vest le tricot de corps
vet le/la vétérinaire
via par
video la vidéo
video recorder le magnétoscope
view la vue
viewfinder le viseur
villa la villa
village le village
vinegar le vinaigre
vineyard le vignoble
visa le visa
visit la visite; *(verb)* visiter; *(someone)* rendre visite à
vitamins les vitamines *fpl*
voice la voix
voltage le voltage

W

waist la taille
wait attendre; **wait for me!** attendez-moi !
waiter le garçon; *see RESTAURANTS*
waiting room la salle d'attente
waitress la serveuse; *see RESTAURANTS*

wake up *(someone)* réveiller; *(oneself)* se réveiller*
Wales le Pays de Galles
walk la promenade; *(verb)* aller à pied; **to go for a walk** aller* se promener
walking boots les chaussures de marche *fpl*
walkman *(tm)* le walkman *(tm)*
wall le mur
wallet le porte-feuille
want vouloir; **I want** je veux; **he wants** il veut; **do you want …?** voulez-vous … ?; *see PRESENT TENSE*
war la guerre
warden *(hostel)* le directeur, la directrice
warehouse l'entrepôt
warm chaud; **it's warm** il fait chaud
warn avertir
warning l'avertissement *m*
warning triangle le triangle de présignalisation
wash laver; *(oneself)* se laver*
washbasin le lavabo
washer *(for bolt etc)* le joint
washing la lessive
washing machine la machine à laver
washing powder la lessive
washing-up la vaisselle
washing-up liquid le produit de vaisselle
wasp la guêpe
watch *(for time)* la montre; *(verb)* regarder; *(take care of)* faire attention à
water l'eau *f*
waterfall la cascade

waterproof imperméable; (*watch etc*) étanche
waterski(ing) le ski nautique
wave (*in sea*) la vague; (*in hair*) l'ondulation *f*
way: this way (*like this*) comme ceci; **can you tell me the way to the ...?** pouvez-vous m'indiquer comment aller à ... ?; *see DIRECTIONS*
we nous
weak faible
weather le temps; **the weather's good** il fait beau; *see WEATHER*
weather forecast la météo
wedding le mariage
Wednesday le mercredi
week la semaine
weekend le week-end
weight le poids
welcome! bienvenue!; **you're welcome** je vous en prie
well bien; **he's well/not well** il va bien/mal; *see SURPRISE*
well done (*meat*) bien cuit
wellingtons les bottes de caoutchouc *fpl*
Welsh gallois
Welshman le Gallois
Welshwoman la Galloise
west l'ouest *m*; **west of** à l'ouest de
wet mouillé
what? quoi ?; **what's that?** qu'est-ce que c'est ?; **what car?** quelle voiture ?
wheel la roue
wheelchair le fauteuil roulant

when quand
where où
which? quel?
while pendant que
whipped cream la crème Chantilly
whisky le whisky
whisper chuchoter
white blanc *m*, blanche *f*
Whitsun les fêtes de la Pentecôte *fpl*
who qui
whole entier
whooping cough la coqueluche
why pourquoi
wide large
wide-angle lens l'objectif grand-angle *m*
widow la veuve
widower le veuf
wife la femme
wild sauvage
will *see FUTURE*
win gagner
wind le vent
window la fenêtre
window seat le siège près de la fenêtre
window shopping le lèche-vitrine
windscreen le pare-brise
windscreen washer le lave-glace
windscreen wiper l'essuie-glace *m*
windsurfing la planche à voile
windy: it's windy il y a du vent
wine le vin; **red/white/rosé wine** le vin rouge/blanc/rosé
wine list la carte des vins

wing (*bird, plane, car*) l'aile *f*
wing mirror le rétroviseur
winter l'hiver *m*
winter sports les sports
   d'hiver *mpl*
wire le fil de fer; (*electrical*)
   le fil électrique
wiring diagram le schéma
   électrique
wish: best wishes meilleurs
   vœux; *see WISHES*
with avec
without sans
witness le témoin
woman la femme
wonderful merveilleux
wood le bois
wool la laine
word le mot
work le travail; (*verb*)
   travailler; **it's not**
   working ça ne marche pas
works (*factory etc*) l'usine *f*
world le monde
worry le souci; **to worry**
   about se faire* du souci
   pour; **don't worry** ne
   vous en faites pas
worse pire
worst: the worst le/la pire
wrap emballer
wrapping paper le papier
   d'emballage
wrench la clé anglaise
wrist le poignet
write écrire
write-off: it's a write-off
   (*car*) elle est fichue
writing paper le papier à
   lettre
wrong faux; **he's wrong** il
   se trompe

X

X-ray la radio

Y

yacht le yacht
year l'année *f*
yellow jaune
yellow pages les pages
   jaunes *fpl*
yes oui; **oh yes I do!** mais
   si!
yesterday hier; *see DAYS*
yet: not yet pas encore
yoghurt le yaourt
you vous; (*familiar*) tu;
   with you avec vous/toi; *see*
   PRONOUNS
young jeune
your votre, vos; (*familiar*)
   ton, ta, tes; *see*
   POSSESSIVES
yours le/la vôtre; (*familiar*)
   le tien, la tienne; *see*
   POSSESSIVES
youth hostel l'auberge de
   jeunesse *f*

Z

zero zéro
zip la fermeture éclair
zoo le zoo
zoom lens le zoom